29

Bess & Harry

BESS & HARRY

AN AMERICAN LOVE STORY

JHAN ROBBINS

G. P. Putnam's Sons
NEW YORK

B
Truman

The author gratefully acknowledges permission from the following
sources to reprint material in their control:
    Coward, McCann & Geoghegan, Inc., for material from *Hail to the
Chiefs* by Ruth Montgomery. Copyright © 1970 by Ruth Montgomery.
    The Kansas City Star Company for material from *The Kansas City
Star* 6/3/35.

LIBRARY OF CONGRESS CATALOGING IN PUBLICATION DATA

Robbins, Jhan.
    Bess and Harry.

    Bibliography: p.
    1. Truman, Harry S., Pres. U. S. 1884–1972—Family.
2. Truman, Bess Wallace. 3. Presidents—United States—
Biography. 4. Presidents—United States—Wives—Biography.
I. Title.
E814.R64   1980   973.918′092′2 [B]   80-13025
ISBN 0-399-12443-8

PRINTED IN THE UNITED STATES OF AMERICA

Second Impression

To Sallie Prugh Robbins

Acknowledgments

THERE ARE MANY people to whom I'm grateful. Margaret Truman Daniel heads the list. I've known her for a number of years and feel for her affection and respect. She shared with me many poignant moments in the lives of her parents, and much of her insight. Another person who helped immeasurably was the late Ethel Noland. I first met the no-nonsense Truman cousin in 1950. I still remember her saying to me, "Mr. Robbins, you see this pencil? Well, if you dare to print a lot of silly foolishness about Harry and Bess, I'll bend it around your head!" I didn't think she was kidding, but apparently she approved of what I wrote and talked with me many more times.

I also want to thank Jacqueline Kennedy Onassis, Lady Bird Johnson, Betty Ford, Rosalynn Carter, Rose Kennedy, John W. Snyder, Major General Harry Vaughan, Mrs. Herbert H. Haukenberry, Mrs. George P. Wallace, Mr. and Mrs. Clark Clifford, Mrs. Dean Acheson, Katie Louchheim, Clifton Daniel, Charles S. Murphy, Alex Petrovic, J. B. West, Lillian Rogers Parks, Mrs. Oscar Chapman, Eleanor and Grace Minor, Mrs. Thomas Twyman, Mrs. Max Truitt, Drucie Snyder Horton, Jane Lingo, Mary Shaw Branton, Reathel M. Odum, Mrs. Fred M.

Vinson, Mrs. Edward Jacobson, Edward P. Meisburger, Eugene P. Donnelly, McKinley Wooden, Francis G. McGowan, Margaret Klapthor, Betty Daniel, Pauline Krueger, Rose Zarwitz, W. Averell Harriman, Barbara L. Heiler, Paul Kupferman, Harold J. Manning, Kenneth V. Bostian and all the others who were interviewed and whose names appear in this book.

I am profoundly grateful to Dr. Benedict K. Zobrist, director of the Harry S. Truman Library, and his outstanding staff. Also my thanks to the dedicated librarians at the Columbia University Oral History Project, the Library of Congress, the Washington *Star,* the Washington *Post,* the Independence *Examiner* and the Kansas City *Star* for their generous help.

I am obligated to various reporters, working and retired, for furnishing me with dozens of Bess-and-Harry anecdotes. I'm eternally in their debt and promise to buy the next round at the National Press Club.

Finally, my appreciation to June Reno, who applied her editing expertise; my researchers, Amy Becker, Pamela Hayes, Marilyn Powell; and my typist, Margaret Glassman.

CONTENTS

PREFACE

"Without Bess's thumb constantly pointing the way, it's very likely that Harry wouldn't have become President of the United States," acknowledged Ethel Noland, Truman's first cousin and the family historian. "Very few outsiders can possibly realize how heavily he counted on her for help. 'Bess,' always 'Bess.' If ever there was a true partnership, those two were it."

Most of the old-timers I talked to in Independence, Missouri, the Trumans' home town, shared this point of view. In the Sandwich U restaurant on West Maple, I was told that when Harry was sworn in as thirty-third President and automatically became one of the most powerful and important men in the world, a wise-cracking native prophesied, "Now we'll be getting a Mom-and-Pop Presidency—two for the price of one. A real bargain!"

A long-time Truman neighbor who had been present when the remark was made said, "It may sound to you like some silly kind of joke. To us it was an affectionate statement that presented the gospel truth. In a few words it told exactly what we were surely in for!"

In Independence, Bess Wallace Truman was rated a very remarkable person. Everybody knew that Harry sought and

1

respected her "let's-see-what-it-really-means" counsel—and that she wasn't reluctant to give it. In the sophisticated circles of Washington, D.C., and New York, she did not fare so well. Eleanor Roosevelt was a hard act to follow. A newspaper columnist labeled Bess dull, dumpy and distant. But her neighbors rushed to her defense. The town's mayor dismissed the comment as being the "imbecile scribbling of a know-nothing writer."

After all, weren't they in a superior position to realize how ridiculous the description was? During his terms as Jackson County judge and United States senator, Harry, whose syntax was occasionally offbeat, had repeatedly told them, "I never make a decision unless the Madam is in on them."

True, like most of the country, Independence residents had been amazed by Harry's astounding Presidential victory in 1947. Their biggest surprise, however, had occurred twenty-eight years before when Bess and Harry stood in front of the mahogany altar at Trinity Episcopal Church and exchanged marriage vows.

"We thought the wedding would never come off," said Matilda Brown, their high school English teacher. "Not that they didn't seem to love each other, but hardly ever have two such extreme opposites wed. Bess was rich, pretty, athletic—a tennis champion—with fine breeding. Harry was much further down the social scale, wore heavy glasses because of very weak eyes, didn't engage in sports, was such a voracious book reader that some considered him a sissy. She was an unabashed tomboy for most of her youth."

Yet for more than five decades, these two "extreme opposites" achieved a uniquely romantic personal life and a vigorous, harmonious, productive political partnership. On their golden wedding anniversary the eighty-five-year-old former President repeated a statement he had made in his memoirs. "She had golden curls," Truman sentimentalized. "And has to this day the most beautiful blue eyes. We went to Sunday school, public school from the fifth grade through high school in the same class, and marched down life's road together. For me she still has the blue eyes and golden hair of yesteryear."

Perhaps the leading Bess booster is her only child, Margaret Daniel. "I suppose it's natural," she said, "that daughters speak well of their mothers—especially in public. But in this instance it stems from a good deal more than mere loyalty. After years of extremely close observation, I've come to the conclusion that my father had to be exceptional. What other kind of man would an exceptional woman like Bess Wallace have chosen for a husband?"

My introduction to this remarkable couple was hallmarked by a veal cutlet—a very inedible one. It began in a Nyack, New York, restaurant when an overzealous waitress insisted that I finish everything on my plate. "What's the matter?" she asked belligerently. "You don't like it?"

I had sat at her table before and knew that uneaten food brought on her instant, offended wrath. The veal cutlet was very, very tough, and when I was sure she wasn't looking, I stuffed it into my tobacco pouch. At the time I was writing an investigative article about national defense, and usually when I'm working on a major story, I refrain also from pipe smoking. I promptly forgot the incident.

A few days later the first of several meetings scheduled in Washington, D.C., was with General Hoyt Vandenberg, President Truman's air force chief. As we shook hands, I noticed a pipe on his desk and offered him some tobacco. Courteously he accepted the pouch, unzipped it, looked in—and staggered.

I suddenly remembered the veal cutlet and was in the midst of a lame-sounding explanation—"You see, I didn't want to hurt the waitress's feelings"—when his secretary told him that he had a call from the President. Vandenberg listened attentively to the commander in chief, said yes and no several times, then proceeded to tell him about the strange contents of the tobacco pouch. Although I was sitting about five feet from the phone, I could plainly hear laughter at the other end. Each time the volume rose, the general would stare at me strangely and cover his mouth. I was grateful when the interview was over.

Later that afternoon I had an appointment with President Truman, and as I entered the Oval Office, he leaned over slightly and said, "So you're the writer fellow who smokes that exotic tobacco. I've been wanting to get a look at you!"

Again I tried to offer an excuse, but he stopped me. "Young fellow," he said, "never apologize if you think you're in the right, no matter how damn foolish you seem. If you like puffing away on a meat blend, stick to your guns. Ever think about adding salt and pepper to the mixture? Wait till I tell the Missus about it!"

That meeting led to an invitation to attend a White House reception for the French ambassador. As I walked down the receiving line, Truman introduced me to his wife. "Remember," he told her, "I spoke to you about this guy. His writing is okay, but when it comes to tobacco, he has some mighty peculiar tastes."

Bess smiled shyly, studied me for a moment, then extended her hand. She said, "Do you still favor that pipe mixture?" Then she laughed good-naturedly.

Each time I saw her after that, she'd remind me of the tobacco-pouch episode, but not in an unkind way. She would also inquire as to what I had been doing recently and sounded as if she really wanted to know. I had firsthand experience of how her sensitivity was quickly transferred to Harry. It occurred when Norman Cousins, then editor of *Saturday Review,* arranged to bring the Hiroshima Maidens, a small group of Japanese girls maimed by the atom bomb, to the United States for plastic surgery. My Quaker Meeting in Wilton, Connecticut, provided housing for two of the maidens, Suzue Oshima and Misako Kanabe. They lived in my house for part of the eighteen months they were treated at New York's Mt. Sinai Hospital.

They wanted to meet Truman, and I introduced them to the former President during a visit he and Bess made to New York City. The girls had been children when the bomb was dropped, but with typical Japanese diffidence they tried to explain in their stumbling English how sorry they were for all the terrible harm the Japanese had inflicted upon our country. They apologized for Pearl Harbor—they had been eight years old in 1941.

Truman listened to them, nodded and said bluntly, "I'm not sorry I used the bomb. I'd do it again."

Suzue, whose left arm was attached temporarily to her abdomen for skin-grafting purposes, started to giggle agitatedly. Misako, her face obscured by a large bandage, also began to giggle. Truman was astonished, but Bess quickly sensed that the giggles meant discomfort. (In Japan giggling often expresses embarrassment or helplessness rather than amusement.) Although she rarely showed affection in public, Bess put her arms around Suzue and said, "How horrible war is."

A chagrined Truman looked at his wife and murmured weakly, "Yes, it is. I'm truly sorry it caused you such a hurt."

That may have been the very moment I started thinking about writing this book. I saw the Trumans frequently and found myself growing intrigued by this supposedly-very-different-from-each-other-couple. I had the occasion to interview dozens of their intimates as, over the years, I wrote numerous Truman articles (the President included one of them in his volume, *Mr. Citizen*).

When I began gathering additional material, I feared that much oral history had been lost, as the sources had died. Not so. I quickly discovered that many Truman confidants had delighted in relating Bess-and-Harry anecdotes to their offspring. Better still, I found that many Truman relatives, friends and associates are long-lived and still very articulate.

I—or one of my researchers—spoke to hundreds of people. So many that Margaret once said, "Jhan, you should be made an honorary member of the Truman clan. You know more about us than we do."

This book is about Bess and Harry as friends, lovers and political comrades. It is also about Bess herself, who obstinately selected a most unlikely man, tenderly and skillfully helped him to the White House at a historical moment and treated it all like a pleasant bridge game, well played and nicely won.

—Jhan Robbins

I INDEPENDENT INDEPENDENCE

INDEPENDENCE, THE SEAT of Jackson County, in west-central Missouri, was settled in 1827. It is best known today as the home of Harry S. Truman, although he was born twenty miles away in Lamar, Missouri. Most stores and offices display large photographs of the late President. Everything in the vicinity seems to be named after him: Truman Medical Center, Truman Used Furniture, Truman Auto Body, Truman Draw Bridge, Truman Cafeteria, Truman Self Service Laundry, Truman Road, Truman Senior High, Truman Health Room, Truman Book Shop, Truman Shopping Center.

Time was when Independence was recognized for something else. Independence was the last major point where wagon trains gathered for their long trek across the plains. It was a jumping-off point for the Santa Fé, Oregon and California trails. In the mid-nineteenth century the once-sleepy village became a noisy, rich and lively town where pioneer families struggled for turns to become part of wagon companies that were westbound beyond the Rockies. News of gold discovered in California brought additional get-rich-quick migrants.

During the peak of frontier travel, there were often more than five thousand visitors in one night. The town got so packed that one resident said, "From morning until night the streets are crowded with people from all parts of the U.S. It's next to impossible to drive a carriage through our principal streets. . . . The more adventurous souls sample the Independence alcohol drink, better known as skull varnish. It's made of straight corn whiskey and blackstrap molasses."

The bedlam didn't last. The roads in Independence were in bad shape, and travelers discovered that nearby Westport was a much better place to begin their journey. As a result, the town was bypassed and for a brief period in the early 1860s enjoyed a tranquil recess.

"Although most of the migrants had departed, they left their stamp behind," said Alex Petrovic, a former Jackson County judge who held the same court seat Harry once occupied. "Succeeding generations felt their impact of strength, determination and spunk."

When Fort Sumter was fired upon and the War Between the States began, Independence sprang to life again. Many of the residents had come from Kentucky, Tennessee and Virginia and were partial to the South. The feeling lingers on, and handkerchiefs still wave when the band plays "Dixie." Once Harry, dressed in his blue national guard uniform, visited his grandmother. Being nearsighted, she mistook him at a distance for a Yankee and ordered him to leave at once.

During the Civil War years guerrilla bands raided the countryside, robbing wagon trains, destroying bridges, firing on railroad trains, harassing federal troops. These lawless brigades were often supported by the town's Southern sympathizers. Yet despite their strong feelings they were more moderate than many of their Southern neighbors. That fact didn't stop the federal government from issuing the infamous "Order No. 11," which directed the

burning of a thirty-mile strip of land on the Missouri side of
the Kansas border so that the raiding parties of the
irregulars would be forced out into the open.

Longtime Independence dwellers, including Truman's
forebears, were ordered to leave and allowed to take only
what they could carry. Then Union soldiers set torches to
their homes and barns. Most of the displaced families spent
the war years with relatives in the deep South. Others
wandered from one temporary shelter to the next. Only
after Lee's surrender at Appomattox were they permitted
reentrance.

They came back to watch enviously the rapid expansion
of Kansas City, less than ten miles away, as it drastically
overtook their town in growth and importance. For the next
several decades they sat on their wicker porch rockers and
sadly reflected on their turbulent history: Queen City of the
trails . . . important stop for the Mormon movement and
migration to the Great Salt Lake . . . site of some of the
bloodiest conflicts of the Civil War . . . where Wild Bill
Hickok got his nickname . . . burial ground of Jim Bridger,
who discovered the first pathways through the Rockies . . .
site of the prison that once housed William Quantrill, Cole
Younger and Frank James.

"That jail furnished Harry with one of his favorite yarns,"
said Major General Harry Vaughan, Truman's close friend
and former military aide. "That man sure was a born
storyteller. He'd look you straight in the eye, point a finger
upward, grin and then start in. I can still hear him telling
this one: 'It seems that a kinsman of Jesse James had been
accused of stealing another man's horse—the most dreadful
crime in these parts. The culprit was found guilty and given
a stiff sentence, but at Christmastime the kind-hearted
warden released him on parole in order that he might spend
the holidays with his aged and ailing mother. He promised
faithfully that he would return on New Year's day.

"'The warden wasn't disappointed—on January 1, 1883,

exactly at the appointed hour, the prisoner galloped back to jail—*riding a stolen horse!'*

"One time Bess was around as he told the story. She always had a delightful sense of humor and added her own punch line when he finished: 'I guess in Independence even the robbers are honest!'"

In 1948 and succeeding years the town annexed new territory many times its size and more than doubled its population, which is now 120,000. However, Independence is really two communities, and most of the residents refer to them simply as Old Town and New Town. One ancient resident said sadly, "Not too long ago the folks living in New Town were taller than their trees!"

In the Victorian-era part, families have lived in the same large houses trimmed with carpenter-Gothic gingerbread for generations. People are still close-knit, and friendships date back to childhood. "There are a great many cousins in Independence," Bess said. "Those that aren't mine seem to be related to Harry."

Most people in the older section go to church on Sunday. A large number attend Mormon services, and the world headquarters of the Reorganized Church of Jesus Christ of Latter Day Saints is located in Independence. The midday meal is "dinner," and families return from worship to what is likely to be a large platter of fried chicken, corn fritters, greens and apple pie topped with homemade ice cream. A handshake is still a sufficient contract, men tip their hats and outside doors are rarely locked.

"Many of the scenes are so intrinsically American," said Eleanor Minor, an Old Town native and childhood friend of Bess, "they could have been painted by Norman Rockwell. Independence is probably like hundreds of other places. But there is a major difference. We're only a few miles from a thriving metropolis, and therefore we have the best of two worlds—small-town simplicity and the culture of a big city."

The President's home at 219 North Delaware was an

Independence showplace long before it became known as
the Summer White House, which new arrivals called the
Hyde Park of the Middle West. Longtime residents still
refer to it as the Gates House. It was lovingly built by
George Porterfield Gates, Bess's maternal grandfather, who
brought his family to Independence from Lunenburg, Ver-
mont, in the early 1860s.

Gates founded the first commercial flour mill in Missouri.
He advertised that his Queen of the Pantry flour would
make the best hot biscuits in the world. Evidently, west-of-
the-Mississippi housewives believed him, and the mill pros-
pered. Soon he was one of the wealthiest men in town.

The Gates house is a rambling, three-story, white frame
structure with wide verandas, gingerbread gables and
stained-glass windows. It has fourteen large rooms, with a
center hall and a dark walnut stairway. The hall is flanked
on the right by an old-fashioned double parlor. On the left
is the music room. Across the back of the house is a huge
dining room whose antique mahogany table can be extended to seat thirty guests. The furnishings include much
interesting old furniture, some of which came to Independence in a wagon train with Mrs. Truman's ancestors.

"To be invited to a Gates party was one of the highest
honors you could receive," said a neighbor. "Everything
was done just so, and there were servants all over the place.
Bess comes by her impeccable manners quite naturally."

The Truman family lived in much more modest surroundings. Harry's father, John Anderson Truman, nicknamed
Peanuts because of his short stature, had been a hardwork-
ing mule trader. "He worked from daylight to dark all the
time," recalled his son. In 1890 John Truman moved the
family from his father-in-law's six-hundred-acre farm to
Independence, twenty miles away. For $1,000 down and a
$3,000 mortgage, he purchased a modest house on South
Chrysler Street. John, who had little formal education, was

an unusually taciturn man who deferred most major decisions to his more domineering wife. Martha Ellen Truman was not the rustic hayseed that she was often portrayed as being. She had graduated from Baptist Female College in Lexington, Missouri, and was convinced that a more settled community was preferable to a farm as a place to raise their children.

Harry said, "When I was six, Vivian three, and Mary one year old, we moved to Independence. Mama was anxious we should have town schooling."

The Independence school system had long been regarded as one of the best in the Midwest. "Pendergast's notorious political machine ruled Jackson County with an iron fist," said Alec Petrovic, former Jackson County judge and lifetime resident of the area. "But they only put a few fingers on education. I guess they knew that the Independence voter would get all riled up if they tampered a great deal with the schools. Like most bosses who want to have a long reign, the Pendergasts instinctively knew when to draw back."

Truman, who had entered Jackson County politics under the Pendergast aegis, once compared Joseph Stalin to him. After meeting the Soviet dictator in Potsdam, Harry said, "He was as near Tom Pendergast as any man I knew."

T.J., as the ward heelers affectionately called the political boss, had succeeded his elder brother Jim Pendergast, who founded the dynasty. Soon, however, T.J. had gained more absolute power than Jim had ever dreamed of. He was the acknowledged leader of Jackson County and eventually of a large part of the state.

He looked the part of a kingmaker. Cartoonists who had dubbed him Boss Tweed Reincarnated delighted in sketching his tiny black derby, which he always wore slightly askew on his massive bald head. His tremendous bull neck, his pot belly and long, hairy, back-slapping arms completed the cartoon. Cigar ashes constantly drifted down to his lapels, and he suffered from a bad case of body odor.

A neighbor once remarked to Madge Wallace, Bess's mother, "Tom Pendergast always looks as if he's hurting from a bad stomachache."

To which Mrs. Wallace is reputed to have replied, "Also from a perpetual case of bad manners and body stench!"

Pendergast controlled all party nominations and party patronage, profited extravagantly from tax favors, openly bought votes. He explained his success to a *New York Times* reporter. "I'm the boss," he said. "The reason I'm the boss is because of my ability. . . . I know how to select ward captains and I know how to get the poor. Every one of my workers has a fund to buy food, coal, shoes and clothing. When a poor man comes to old Tom's boys for help, we don't make one of those damn fool investigations like those city charities. No, by God, we fill his belly and warm his back and vote him our way."

What Pendergast couldn't buy, armed goons did. An Associated Press story said: "Big Tom Pendergast's Democratic machine rode to overwhelming victory today after a blood-stained election marked by four killings, scores of sluggings and machine gun terrorists."

"Independence residents were horrified by Pendergast's tactics," said Petrovic. "They kept hoping it can't happen here. Thank God it didn't!"

II NORMAN ROCKWELL CHILDHOODS

ETHEL NOLAND, TRUMAN's plump, half-placid, half-cantankerous first cousin, went through school with Bess and Harry and, as she put it, "watched them grow up and form character."

She said, "From birth on they were each provided with love and security—which the experts tell us build self-respect. Bess and Harry learned moral values through example and rule. Home life at the Wallaces' was perhaps more formal. The Trumans didn't have so much time for gracious living, but under both roofs everyone knew right from wrong and no mistake. By the time they were teenagers—the age when most of us begin to show the stuff we're made of—Bess and Harry each displayed a firm set of moral values."

Reminiscing in her sixties, Bess recalled her and her three brothers' childhood as "blissful." She told Ethel Noland, "There were disappointments and some arguments, of course. Once my mother had a dress made for me that was a rather violent shade of red and I despised it—refused to wear it. My mother didn't scold me or reproach me, tell me I was spoiled or ungrateful. She just hung it up in the closet and said nothing. A few weeks later I wore it to church and everyone said how nice I looked. I felt like a fool.

"For forgetting my manners or other misdemeanors, I was punished, but never physically and never in anger. I forgot to water some houseplants that my grandfather especially prized. They withered and one died. As penalty, I was made to go to my room and practice doing bound buttonholes, which I hated. There was never much praise for things well done—that was expected of me."

Humor shared with adults in the family brought Harry Truman to an appreciation of values. "My first memory," he said, "is that of chasing a frog around the backyard in Cass County, Missouri. Grandmother Young watched the performance and thought it very funny that a two-year-old could slap his knee and laugh so loudly at a jumping frog . . . Yet she was careful to caution me not to hurt the frog."

Harry was sixty-eight when he recalled the incident. "I had just the happiest childhood that could ever be imagined," he said. "If I slouched on some chore, like not stripping a cow's udder properly, I got a swift kick in the rear, but mostly I was shown, not told, how to behave. I never heard anyone in my family lie . . . In those days, in the time I was growing up, people thought more of an honest man than any one thing. If a man wasn't honest, he wouldn't stay long in the neighborhood. They would run him out. These were the qualities I was taught that are most important and I tried to follow them when I was President."

Truman biographers may differ sharply in assessing his White House actions—but not his wife's. No one who ever met Mrs. Truman ever doubted her unimpeachable character. Even the hysterical witch-hunter Joe McCarthy, who insisted that Truman coddled Communists in the government, had kind words for her. The junior senator from Wisconsin ranted, "The son of a bitch should be impeached." But he also told a reporter, "Harry showed good judgment when he picked Bess. She's the only good thing about the White House."

The families of Bess and Harry traveled in different social circles in Independence. Truman's relatives are quick to call attention to the nine hundred acres of prime Missouri topsoil they owned, which certainly made them socially acceptable. But Truman pointed out that his family was not very prosperous. "We never did catch up with our debts," he said. "We always owed the bank something—sometimes more, sometimes less—but we always owed the bank . . . That was back in the days when owing the bank was something you tried to keep secret. It was not a way of life like now."

For all the long years that Bess and Harry "kept company," the two families are not known to have had tea or broken bread together. The Trumans didn't have time to stop for tea—they were grab-a-cup-of-coffee people. But there is little doubt that they shared similar values.

On one occasion Harry's father was called as a witness in a lawsuit. The opposing attorney tried frantically to shake his testimony, but despite some very bombastic questioning, John Truman stuck to the same story. Finally, in desperation, the lawyer said, "Now, John, you know that's a damn lie!" Whereupon John Truman jumped out of the witness box and chased the lawyer clear out of the courthouse.

A similar episode reflects the deep-rooted moral philosophy of Bess's maternal grandfather, George Porterfield Gates. Although he employed a great many people in his mill, he took a personal interest in every phase of its daily operation. One day a customer from nearby Westport, Missouri, was slightly overcharged. Gates was furious when he heard about the transaction, and as the man's carriage rounded the corner, the perspiring and puffing Gates overtook him and thrust the proper change into his hand.

When one of the Gates's servants told eleven-year-old Bess about the incident, her matter-of-fact reply was, "Well, wasn't the man charged too much? What else could grandfather do?"

Bess was never allowed to forget her heritage as granddaughter of one of the town's leading citizens. Gates passed down his strict patrician code to his daughter. Madge Gates was often called the queenliest woman Independence ever produced.

A whimsical story is told about her haughtiness: One day Bess's mother and a friend were crossing Independence's Main Street when a runaway horse came galloping by. As usual, Madge had her nose high in the air; the fast-moving mount stepped in a mud puddle and splattered her carefully selected dress. Madge was indignant and burst out sharply, "Of all the insolence! Doesn't he know who I am?" Marriage to David Willock Wallace, a local youth who seemed destined for success, just enhanced her illusions of grandeur.

Somehow Bess didn't inherit this idiosyncrasy. In many ways she seemed to favor her father. "He was very handsome and greatly admired," said Henry Chiles, former treasurer of Jackson County. "Dave Wallace was something of a child prodigy. He was the most popular man I ever knew and the most promising man of the county. Led all the parades. Especially on the Fourth of July. He had a big riding horse."

Wallace had been an assistant docket clerk of the Missouri State Senate when he was only fourteen years old. After graduating from college, he was employed as deputy county recorder and then transferred himself to the U.S. Customs Office in Kansas City. At the age of thirty-one he had been unanimously elected as Eminent Commander of the Knights of Templar of Missouri, a highly esteemed and influential fraternal order. "A lot of people felt that one day Dave Wallace might even be elected governor," Chiles said. "He was the kind of man that any child would be proud to have as a parent."

Bess was much attached to her father. Her quick wit, keen sense of humor, hearty laugh and warm friendliness came from him. She often spoke of the "carefree days" that he made possible. She told Ethel Noland, "He made life in Independence just one lovely adventure after the other. He'd suggest wonderful things to do. He even made the games we played exciting adventures."

A favorite was Run Sheep Run, a version of hide-and-seek where the team leader gives hand signals for when to emerge and safely dash to home base. Other popular games were variations of Fox and Dogs and Mother, May I?

The children on Delaware Street where the Wallaces lived and in all the rest of the well-to-do parts of the community would be called in late afternoon to wash up and change their clothes. In the summer the girls put on starched dotted-swiss dresses with pink sashes and would go to the lawn to greet their fathers when they arrived from their offices. The importance of looking nice for their male parents was impressed on them very early.

After supper the entire family would walk down to Mr. Bostian's Ice Cream Parlor on the square. Bess's favorite treat was a sundae that her friend, Elizabeth Paxton Forsling, originated. It was known as a Black and Tan—gobs of homemade chocolate ice cream covered with rich caramel syrup. As the children ate their desserts, Mr. Bostian, the former postmaster, entertained them with fascinating tales about the James brothers, Cole Younger and William Quantrill, the Civil War raider.

"All around the town of Independence were beautiful forests where a child might wander," Mrs. Forsling recalled. "Of course when we were children, there were no automobiles, there were no hot rods tearing up and down the street, no screeching of rubber tires. It was the gas-jet age, a lovely age of innocence; the Gay Nineties were in full bloom."

During that period it was unusual for a girl to excel in athletics. Bess did. She had to, growing up with three younger brothers. Harry Chiles said, "Physically, Bess could do whatever she wanted to. She was just as good a ball player as her brothers were, and they knew it. She was quite a tomboy."

An anecdote revolves around that "tomboy" designation. It took place in the final inning of an all-boy sandlot baseball game. Bess was about thirteen years old at the time. She was on her way to a dancing class, all dressed up in a freshly starched blue ruffled dress and brand new black patent leather pumps. Along the way she stopped to watch her brothers' team take a beating. They were three runs behind and it was the last inning. Somehow they managed to fill the bases. That was when Bess was called in to pinch-hit.

"Yes, she made a home run," said Miss Noland. "Yes, she soiled her pretty dress as she scampered along the dusty baselines. And, yes, she got to the dance class a bit late— but with a lovely explanation: 'It would be a poor kind of a sister that wouldn't help a brother in need!'"

In addition to baseball, Bess was skilled in skating, swimming, tennis, hunting and fishing. "Her coordination was wonderful," said Mrs. Herbert H. Haukenberry, one of Harry's cousins, who lives in a small frame house directly opposite the late President's home. Mrs. Haukenberry, a retired Kansas City third-grade teacher, has the unmistakable look of a Truman.

"Bess could also beat most boys in mumblety-peg and marble shooting," she said. "My mother told me she was allowed to drive the family's horse and buggy. Her ability with horses was well known, as she was considered an excellent rider. She could put a horse over a big pasture fence. But don't get the idea that Bess was all tomboy. At times she was very feminine. She had a pair of greyhounds that she used to walk. My mother would say how fine a figure she cut. I suppose her stylish ways were far off from what Harry was accustomed to."

The Truman family moved from Solomon Young's farm to Independence when Harry was six years old. One of the first things the boy's mother did was take him to Sunday school. "He never forgot that visit," Mrs. Haukenberry said. "That's when he first saw Bess. He often spoke about that initial meeting with a very pretty and well-dressed blonde little girl named Elizabeth Virginia Wallace. I suppose in many ways it was the most important day of his life and may well have changed it. Who knows? Without Bess, he might have been just another farmer."

Just before the move to Independence, Harry's mother noticed that he was bumping into the piano and had trouble distinguishing the notes she was teaching him. She took the youngster to an oculist in Kansas City, who fitted Harry with thick-lensed glasses. Diagnosis: "Eyeballs are excessively flat, causing extreme shortsight. Patient is near total blindness."

The glasses were a great help in seeing but a great handicap in playing. "I was carefully cautioned by the eye doctor about breaking my glasses," said Truman. "I was afraid to join in the rough-and-tumble games in the school yard and the back lot. My time was spent reading, and by the time I was thirteen or fourteen years old, I had read all the books in the Independence Public Library and our big old Bible three times through."

Harry may have fretted about having to wear glasses, but that was the feature Bess noticed first. She recalled, "The thing I remember most about him when we were growing up in Independence was those eyeglasses. I thought they rather made him look rakish—as though he might up and do just about anything.''

Truman was once asked if he was admired when he was young. "Why, no," he quickly replied. "I was never popular. The popular boys were the ones who were good at games and had big, tight fists. I was never like that. Without my glasses I was blind as a bat, and to tell the truth I was kind of a sissy. If there was any danger of getting into a fight, I always ran.''

While Harry was busy reading library books and avoiding neighborhood scuffles, Bess was out playing tennis. She loved the game and was considered one of the best players in Independence—male or female. One of her more persistent beaux tried to impress her on the tennis court, but she quickly wore him out. Resting while she challenged another young man, he tried to curry her favor by running after her tennis balls. "I'll shag it for you, Miss Bess," he offered again and again.

"No, thank you!" she finally snapped. "If you don't mind, I'll get my own!"

"Lots of young men tried to woo Bess," Mrs. Haukenberry said. "But I guess she was waiting for Harry. He more than felt that way about her and would consider it a red-letter day if she allowed him to carry her books. When they were in high school, he would come twice a week to my house to be tutored in Latin, not because he needed help but because he knew she would be here. They graduated in 1901, in a class where the smartest student was Charlie Ross, who in Harry's administration was made White House press secretary.''

A short time later Bess's lighthearted adolescence abruptly ended. Her easy-natured father, then forty-three years old, returned from work, sat in the bathtub, and fired a pistol bullet into his head. He had been drinking heavily. Neighbors felt that his suicide had resulted from his being the husband of a woman who constantly reminded him of her exalted social position.

One of them said, "Dave was heavily in debt. He tried so hard to keep up with his wealthy in-laws. He just couldn't. Madge never let him forget it—or who she was. It finally got to him."

"Whatever you do, don't use my name," said another acquaintance. "I don't want to be guilty of saying anything that would hurt Bess, because she's such a fine person. But after he died, she became more reserved. I think her father's suicide made her that way. What I really mean is that it made her more tolerant of other people. Her extreme public shyness seemed to show from then on. She was a tomboy before; almost overnight she became a refined lady—and a fairly retiring one!"

After her father's death, Bess, her brothers, and her widowed mother went to live in the Gates's Delaware Street house. It was quickly decided that grief-stricken Bess should be sent to the very fashionable Barstow Finishing School for Girls in Kansas City, as her mother felt was fitting for a girl of her background.

At the time Harry was desperately hoping to get an appointment to West Point. He soon learned that his poor eyesight would keep him from passing the physical examination. Instead he got a job with the J. L. Smith Construction Company as a timekeeper—$35 a month.

"In those days $35 was considered quite decent money," said Mrs. Haukenberry. "But Harry wasn't overjoyed. Many of his friends were going off to college. He couldn't go because of finances. He wondered if he'd ever amount to anything."

III THE LONGEST COURTSHIP

"BESS HAD A very busy social life," said Truman's cousin, Mrs. Haukenberry. "In those days she was still as slender as a twig, had large blue eyes, and a blanket of very blonde hair. She had more admirers than you could shake a stick at, and most of them were considered tip-top catches. They followed her all over town like little puppies. This didn't make Harry very happy. He was full of beans in most matters, but seemed to suffer from an inferiority complex where she was concerned—that he wasn't good enough for her.

"Bess lived just across the street, and whenever Harry came to see us, he'd talk mainly about her; never did anything about it. During one of his visits, my grandmother said, 'I have a plate that belongs to Mrs. Wallace. She sent over a cake. That will be a good way for you to meet Bess again.' He was so anxious to get across the street with that plate everybody prayed he wouldn't drop it on the way over."

Mrs. Wallace wasn't very impressed by the friendship, and she didn't hide her disapproval. Janey Chiles, a former

Independence schoolteacher, said, "I thought they would never get married. There wasn't anybody in town Mrs. Wallace didn't look down on. And Harry Truman was not at the time a very promising prospect."

Harry's grandfather Solomon Young had died, and John Truman was now running the farm. He asked his son for help. For the next ten years Harry climbed out of bed before dawn, milked cows, fed hogs, plowed, sowed, harrowed, and reaped, as well as practicing the piano and doing a great deal of reading.

"Mrs. Wallace had never been a farm woman," said Mrs. Haukenberry. "She didn't think anyone who tilled the soil could possibly amount to much, and despite Harry's passion for books and music, she still thought of him as a poor dirt-farmer. And what's worse, one who didn't even own the farm he worked."

Before returning to the Young farm, Harry had had a series of town jobs that Mrs. Wallace also felt were uninspiring and without future. In 1903 he found employment as a bank teller. He supplemented his income by working Saturday matinees as an usher at Kansas City's Grand Theater. There is a story that goes with that part-time job. At one performance Bess arrived with a date. The movie house was crowded and pitch-black, but Harry's flashlight swiftly seated the couple—Bess in the tenth row center and her escort in the first row—behind a pole!

Bess continued to attract scores of ardent boyfriends. They would often take her to local balls, where she was regarded as one of the finer dancers. She and a partner were once awarded a prize for their "excellent waltzing."

"I loved to dance better than anything," she said. "I've never been able to teach Harry any steps. He didn't learn in his youth, perhaps because there wasn't much dancing in Baptist circles."

Despite this lack, Truman was elevated to the top of Bess's list.

"The way those two looked at each other," recalled Ethel Noland, "you knew it was bound to happen."

Every Saturday evening Harry would faithfully travel to Independence by train and streetcar. He'd usually carry a small bouquet of roses and violets. "A standard dating custom in Independence," said Miss Noland, "was to take long hikes in the woods. There were many wonderful trails nearby, and Harry and Bess covered them all. They didn't hold hands but they walked very close. Sometimes I don't think you could have seen any open space between them. Bess knew the names of all the wildflowers, and when they returned, she'd tell us what they had seen. Harry was so proud of her knowledge."

Sometimes other couples went along on the nature walks. During one of them a "reverse" race was staged. "Everyone agreed to run backward," she recalled. "For most of the race Bess was well out in front. Suddenly she dropped back and finished behind Harry. I'm sure she did it on purpose, not wanting to appear as a superior runner to Harry."

Another thing they did on dates was go fishing. Rather, it was Bess who was the angler. While she dropped bait and watched the bobbing cork, Harry would sit on the bank beside the tackle box and read to her. One time Bess landed a large perch as he reached the line: "The shoemaker singing as he sits on his bench . . ." (From Walt Whitman's *I Hear America Singing*). He recited it with such gusto that the startled fish got away.

In 1915 Harry bought a five-year-old Stafford convertible, which made commuting easier. It also made distant picnics and outings possible. Cousins, friends, and Bess's brothers, their wives or fiancées usually went along. "Sometimes the car was so full that Harry would have to make as many as three trips in order to transport everyone," Miss Noland said. "He didn't seem to mind as long as Bess accompanied him. He was a fast driver but on those trips he just crawled along at a snail's pace and sneaked stares at Bess perched on the front seat with her fair hair blowing.

"At the time," she recalled, "matchmaking was not unusual. Neighbors of the [John] Trumans told them that their schoolteacher niece was planning to visit them from Ashland, Virginia. They claimed that the girl was pretty and shared a common interest with Harry—she played the piano very well. When the girl came for a visit, the neighbors brought her over. Uncle John said that Harry was wearing his best clothes and acted very proper. He applauded politely when the girl finished playing the piano. But that was all there was to it. He never saw her again. To Harry, who had some Tom Sawyer and Huckleberry Finn in him, Bess was his Becky Thatcher. He just couldn't see anybody else."

Mrs. Haukenberry, Ethel Noland's niece, said, "Even though they were older, we were still close pals. Bess's brother Fred was my age—he and I graduated in the same class in the old Independence High. Fred would encourage Harry to play the piano, and he never needed much coaxing. He preferred classical music, but he'd play rag, romantic—just about everything. He was loads of fun.

"Once we had a picnic at Rock Creek, which is west of here. Unexpectedly, it started raining pitchforks. There was a house under construction and we all ran to it to avoid getting soaked. The window openings were covered with tar paper and it was very dark and spooky inside. That's when we heard the eerie, ghostlike moaning sounds. I don't mind telling you that I was more than a little scared. Then Harry burst into the room, laughing and slapping his sides. He was the ghost!"

Another practical joke that caused a great deal of merriment occurred during an outing on the banks of the Missouri River. Two male members of the party, Ed Green and Fred Colgan, put a note in an empty bottle they found.

They carefully described themselves and enclosed their addresses; then they tossed the bottle into the water.

The next day Harry and a coconspirator posted a letter to Green and Colgan, in which they pretended to be two very pretty young ladies who had discovered the bottle. Amorous notes went back and forth. Soon two thriving romances were in process. Bess felt that perhaps Harry was acting too brashly, but reluctantly she went along with the gag. It was finally halted when it was realized that the two young men were hopelessly in love with imaginary maidens. Green and Colgan found out about the spoof and were so enraged that they didn't speak to Harry for weeks. "I was very grateful to Bess," Truman said later. "Never once did she tell me, 'I told you so!'"

Mrs. Haukenberry has a picture of Bess and Harry that was taken shortly after the bottle episode. "Everything seems to be all right," she said. "They are sitting on the ground in our backyard eating large chunks of watermelon with zest—laughing and spitting seeds. My aunt Ethel had a copy of that photograph, and *Life* magazine wanted it. But she refused to give it to them because she felt Bess didn't look very dignified.

"When he was courting her, he'd spend the night in our house. Don't ask me where he slept. There were eight of us—my grandmother, my grandfather, my mother, my two aunts, and three children. Fortunately, everybody liked him tremendously. We had an upright piano at the time, which stood right against this wall. Before he'd go over to Bess, he'd sit down and play. We'd always ask for more. On Sunday mornings he'd accompany Bess to Trinity Episcopal Church down the street."

Mrs. Thomas Twyman, a very close friend, remembers those church appearances. "Harry was a Baptist, but many's the time he'd go along with Bess to Episcopal services. He'd sit so straight and be so serious. That was

until we started to sing. You'd think he had just heard
Jenny Lind from the way he looked. I sang with Bess and I
fear the results were not very good. Singing was definitely
not our strong point. But you certainly wouldn't think it
from his expression."

Bess enjoyed her choral contribution, even though she
wasn't particularly talented. She and Harry would frequently visit Kansas City's Willis Wood Hall on Eleventh
and Baltimore to hear opera stars. Years later she was
extremely proud of her daughter's voice, and once after a
hugely successful concert, she remarked, "Thank goodness
Margaret doesn't take after me in that department. I sound
like a dying crow when I sing." Then after a slight pause she
modified her statement. "I'm not being very kind to the
crows," she said.

The pleasant and easygoing Bess-Harry relationship went
on for years and would probably have continued for many
more if Woodrow Wilson hadn't declared war. Truman had
been a private in the Second Field Artillery of the Missouri
National Guard. When the United States entered the war,
his unit became part of the regular army, and Harry was
made a first lieutenant.

"He dashed around town wearing his natty uniform,"
said Eddie Jacobson, who was to become Truman's haberdashery partner. "The influence it had on Bess showed
quickly. She wanted to get married at once, but he insisted
on waiting until he returned in one piece. 'I didn't think it
was right,' he tried to explain. 'I don't think it's fair to get
married and maybe come home crippled and have the most
beautiful and sweetest girl in the world tied down.'"

On the first day of spring, 1918, Bess Wallace received a
very early and very passionate long distance phone call from
Rosedale, Kansas. Lieutenant Harry Truman was at the
other end. He was on his way to New York City to be

processed for overseas duty. The other soldiers were fast asleep—not Harry. When the train made the brief stop, Truman quickly asked the switchman if he could call his girl friend in Independence, as he wanted to confirm their engagement.

"Call her," the railroad employee said. "The phone's yours. But if she doesn't break the engagement at four o'clock in the morning, she really loves you."

Obviously she did love him—Bess and Harry were firmly betrothed. However, it had taken the diffident lieutenant more than twenty years to persuade her to say yes. Neighbors claim that they would have been married long before. Harry wanted to. So did Bess. But she was a dutiful daughter who always obeyed her mother.

"Madge Wallace may not have been overly pleased with the news," said Mrs. Haukenberry. "But Harry was beside himself with joy. Bess, too, was thrilled. That is, when she could forget about the war—a pretty difficult thing to do in that period."

She helped form the Independence War Widows, who engaged in such home-front activities as rolling bandages and knitting sweaters for the soldiers. Truman received one of those sweaters, which he proudly showed off—even though the right sleeve was several inches longer than the left.

On July 11, 1918, Harry assumed command of Battery D, 129th Field Artillery, 35th Division. He vividly remembered that day and wrote Bess all about it. Early in the morning the colonel called him in and said he was putting Truman in charge of Battery D, better known as Dizzy D because of its fiercely independent men. Harry explained that it was a most difficult assignment. There had been four commanding officers before him, and none of them could control those wild Irish soldiers.

Eugene Donnelly, a Kansas City attorney and former Battery D corporal, said, "I suppose we were sort of tough, or at least thought so. But almost from the start we discovered that Captain Harry was extremely fair and loyal. He'd go to bat for you if he thought you were being equally honest. I wouldn't be a bit surprised if that was one of the qualities that attracted Bess to him. He was always steadfast to those close to him."

The wartime roster of the battery was approximately 260, but thousands of Missouri men afterward claimed they had served with Dizzy D. Bess once said, "Half the state and to quote Jimmy Durante, 'Everyone wannsa get into da act!'"

Edward Meisburger, a retired newspaperman and legitimate member of the battery, said, "Those two would write to each other every day. I can still see Captain Harry composing a letter to her. It didn't matter if we were in a trench or clear out in the open. We had some pretty rough days—heavy fighting in the Vosges Mountains of Alsace, the St.-Mihiel sector, the Meuse-Argonne offensive, the Somme sector. You name it, it seemed we were there. Through it all he remained calm and continued writing. After a while it got so that Bess became an unofficial member of the battery."

Years later Harry found her destroying those letters in the fireplace. "What are you doing?" he asked.

"I'm burning your letters to me."

"Bess, you oughtn't do that." He was hurt. Aghast.

"Why not? I've read them several times."

"But think of history!"

"I have!"

IV AT LAST A BRIDE

On June 28, 1919, less than two months after Harry's discharge from the army, he and Bess were married. He was thirty-five, she was thirty-four. Although Mrs. Wallace still had strong reservations about Truman's qualities as a son-in-law, she made certain that her daughter would be the loveliest bride the town had ever seen. Bess was elaborately dressed in white georgette with three-quarter-length bell-shaped sleeves, pointed white kid slippers with white enamel buckles, and a white wide-brimmed faille hat. She carried a bouquet of specially grown hothouse rosebuds, baby's breath and fern.

The bridegroom wore a black-and-white checkered suit, and an extremely short army haircut. His sporty, informal clothes and appearance bothered no one but Mrs. Wallace. When she first saw him, she is said to have rolled her eyes to the ceiling of the church and murmured, "Preserve us! Couldn't he at least have borrowed a white linen?"

Dr. John Plunkett, the minister who married the couple, said, "I don't think I have ever seen a more eager groom. During the service he said I do three times—twice when I was just stopping for breath."

Ethel Noland recalled that as the organist played the

Lohengrin "Wedding March," she whispered to one of the
guests that it was customary to speak of how radiant the
bride looks. "Well, in this case," she said, "it is also true of
the groom!"

Just around the corner, Harry's Baptist church had
scheduled another wedding at the exact time, causing a
great deal of confusion among the friends of both couples.
Many of them did not realize their mistake until the wrong
bride and groom marched down the aisle. Bess, who had
been known for her quick-wittedness, said, "I guess some of
them went to the right pew but the wrong church. Do you
suppose I did? I hear that the other bridegroom owns
several buildings and drives a fine-looking automobile."
Then she clutched her new husband's hand and sighed. "I'm
sure I went to the right one!" she said emphatically.
"Shank's mare with Harry would be far better than all the
automobiles in the world!"

It would be nice to say that from that moment on the
Trumans lived happily ever after. Unfortunately, it wasn't
so. Their marriage may have been a splendid one, but it
certainly wasn't all sweetness and light. The Trumans lived
in Mrs. Wallace's home, just as the Roosevelts had lived in
the home of FDR's mother, Mrs. James Roosevelt, at Hyde
Park. It was often done in those days when matriarchs were
stronger; newly married women were thought to need
guidance and external appearances mattered more. Trouble
started soon after a brief honeymoon in Chicago and Port
Huron, Michigan. The couple moved into Bess's house on
North Delaware Street with Mrs. Gates and Mrs. Wallace—
Mr. Gates had died while Harry was overseas. It was a
much grander place than the brand-new husband could
possibly afford—hardly the setting for a dirt farmer. He
chafed because he couldn't pay even half the expenses. It
also meant living with a grandmother-in-law as well as a
mother-in-law.

Almost from the first day some refined, one-sided quib-
bling began. Mrs. Wallace would cut stories out of news-

papers and magazines that depicted the sad plight of the farmer and leave them out on the hall table as if to say, "See what your wife saved you from?" or "See how opportunistically you have handled yourself?"

Harry refused to be quarrelsome. From boyhood on Truman had been known for his ability to mollify. Mrs. Haukenberry recalls that he frequently was asked to settle family disputes. He called the more difficult kinfolk prima donnas. Daughter Margaret feels that a great deal of her father's success with Bess was due to his complete unwillingness to argue.

One of the few complaints Truman ever made about the living arrangement was to Ted Marks, a local tailor and fellow veteran who had been best man at the wedding. He told Marks that sometimes his female in-laws treated him like a "small boy with dirty knees." But when he found it too upsetting, he'd remember his wife. "Suddenly," he said, "everything becomes very worthwhile."

Susan Chiles, an Independence neighbor, remarked, "Harry was always as nice as anyone could be to Mrs. Wallace. It was a most remarkable thing, and I think people around here respect him as much for that as anything else. . . . What really troubled him was finding the right kind of job."

The new Mrs. Truman understood her husband's dilemma in discovering his proper role in the civilian world. She wondered if farming would allow him to display his "special talents," whatever they might be.

"She didn't exactly say no to farming," said Mrs. Haukenberry. "She didn't have to, since it was perfectly clear that she wasn't cut out to be a farmer's wife. Anyway, Harry wasn't cut out to be a farmer. He preferred the way of the city. His brother Vivian was the farmer."

Even with fourteen rooms it was difficult to find privacy, and the couple spent an inordinate amount of time in their bedroom. "The only opportunity he had to be alone with

Bess," said Ted Marks, "was when their bedroom door was shut tight. Bess struggled to give her husband and mother equal time. Believe me, sometimes it required a lot of ingenuity."

On one occasion a local plumber came to repair a leaking kitchen faucet. Harry knew the workman and welcomed him warmly. Mrs. Wallace noticed the hearty greeting. She harrumphed loudly and arched her eyebrows higher than usual. It was very obvious that she didn't approve of her son-in-law's familiarity with the blue-collar worker. Bess quickly came to her husband's rescue and poured coffee for everybody present.

"It's difficult to cross swords when you're sipping blazing coffee," Marks philosophized.

"A few weeks after he was married, Harry and my husband ran into each other on the street," said Mrs. Eddie Jacobson. "The two of them had operated a successful canteen in the army. [The canteen had made a $15,000 profit for the government, which was all but unheard of.] They started to reminisce. It was then that they decided to open up a sort of public canteen—a men's furnishing store."

They resolved to pool all the resources each could get his hands on. Harry raised $15,000 by selling equipment and stock from the farm in which he now had a one-half interest. On November 29, 1919, Truman & Jacobson opened its doors across the street from Kansas City's Muehlebach Hotel. McKinley Wooden, who was a chief mechanic in the 129th Field Artillery, said, "It seemed like an ideal setup—Captain Harry did the selling, Eddie the buying, and Bess kept the books."

She also handled the advertising and was supposedly responsible for a large window sign that read: FOR TRUE VALUE SHOP AT TRUMAN & JACOBSON.

"Many ex-soldiers were returning home and needed new wardrobes," said Thomas McGowan, a former corporal in the Dizzy D Battery. "We used the store as a sort of meeting place."

The owners' army buddies bought dozens of silk shirts and silk hose. Bess urged her friends to recommend the shop to their husbands. She entertained them with accounts of the strange requests Harry often received. One was from a middle-aged woman who wanted a birthday present for her husband.

"What do you suggest?" the woman asked Truman.

"Madam, how about a nice pair of gloves?"

"Capital idea. I believe he wears a size 8½."

"You can exchange them if the size is incorrect. Here are some that just came in."

"They're very nice, but I'm afraid they won't do."

"You're looking at our full winter selection. Pigskin, kid, suede."

"No. They won't do. They've only got five fingers."

"Well, what's wrong with that?"

"Oh, Melvin has six."

Another request caused Bess some astonishment when a customer came in and asked for an "indoor umbrella." It seemed that he had a drip directly above his bed. Rather than have it repaired, he bought an umbrella to protect himself from the trickling water.

Harry felt he should shield his wife from these odd characters and often brought the accounts home for her to work on. Still she had a great deal of spare time, and it was then that she developed her great passion for detective novels. Once Harry looked at the last page of a book Bess was reading and inadvertently blurted out the name of the killer. A furious Bess muttered, "I hope all your customers today ask for six-fingered gloves!"

"When Harry wasn't waiting on trade, you could always find him up in the balcony," recalled Mrs. Jacobson. "He'd have his nose in a book. Law books mostly. Mrs. Truman urged him to study law and later on he went to night law school."

At first Truman & Jacobson did a thriving business. They sold more than $75,000 worth of merchandise and plowed the profits back into the store. "Then old Mellon got in his licks,"* Harry said. "We saw our inventory of $30,000 or $40,000 drop down to about $10,000 value."

"The postwar slump was especially hard on farmers," Truman said. "A bushel of wheat that had sold for $2.15 now brought less than half of the former price. Many of our customers were farmers and they could no longer afford cotton shirts, let alone silk ones at $16 apiece. Instead of buying, the boys came in to ask for loans."

That's when Bess lettered a CLOSED sign and Harry dejectedly hung it on the shop door. Creditors hounded Truman for payment, and he narrowly avoided bankruptcy by returning the remaining stock and agreeing to pay off his share of the indebtedness gradually.

"The Trumans never threw money around," said Miss Noland. "But after the store's collapse, they lived more frugally than ever. They skimped for the next fifteen years to pay off outstanding bills."

Bess rarely spoke of the failure. One of the few public remarks she ever made about it was years later during an automobile ride with Mike Westwood, who often acted as her chauffeur in Independence. It was during an exceedingly gusty storm, and the streets seemed to be paved with broken umbrellas. "We carried umbrellas in the store," she reminisced. "Unfortunately, we didn't sell too many because it never rained like this!"

Several days before Bess had lettered the CLOSED sign, a big Locomobile rolled up to the store. "I was standing

---

* Andrew Mellon was President Harding's secretary of the treasury; many economists charged him with being responsible for the 1920–21 depression. "When you get a man like old Mellon," Truman said, ". . . you've got somebody who'll do everything in his power to make the rich richer and the poor poorer, and that's exactly what happened."

behind the counter feeling blue when Mike Pendergast [the father of one of Truman's wartime buddies] came in," Truman recalled. "'How'd you like to be county judge?' he asked."

There are several versions of this story. Many claim that Truman actively sought the essential backing of the Pendergast machine. All agree, however, that Harry was an ideal candidate: a returning soldier with a local wife who had many voting relatives and influential friends in Jackson County.

Whatever explanation is correct, Harry S. Truman agreed to run and was launched on a new career, and the wisdom of Bess's wish that he use his "special talents" was put to the test.

V THE JUDGE AND THE JUDGE'S WIFE

THE TRUMANS WERE elated at the prospect of Harry becoming a judge. True, he'd not be a jurist in the popular sense and preside over a court of law. The duties were strictly administrative. A county judge in Missouri manages tax money, plans public works, oversees charitable institutions. However, he would be called Judge Truman, and the job did pay *$3600 a year!*

To get the Democratic nomination for any post in Jackson County required the backing of the Pendergast machine, and it had already agreed to support him. To make doubly certain of victory, the Trumans vowed to wage an aggressive campaign. They purchased a dilapidated second-hand Dodge roadster and crisscrossed the county's seven townships. Jointly they canvassed door-to-door, attended picnics and square dances. Bess said, "I heard callers holler Dosey Doe so many times I began thinking Doe was a registered voter!"

Although she was often invited to speak, she would graciously refuse. "A woman's place in public," she told Ethel Noland, "is to sit beside her husband, be silent and be sure her hat is on straight."

Bess cheerfully hewed to that belief, and throughout her husband's long political career, she never formally delivered a campaign speech. The nearest thing to one occurred at an outing in Oak Grove, Missouri, the home of one of Harry's opponents. When the chairman introduced Bess to the crowd, she rose, smiled and said, "You're about to hear from Harry Truman, by far the best man in the race. But then I may be a bit prejudiced since I'm married to him."

She quickly sat down. The applause and whistles that followed indicated that she had made exactly the proper statement. "Bess always had the knack of saying or doing the right thing at the right time," a neighbor said. "When in doubt, she uttered nothing, which takes wisdom, too."

Into even the smallest campaign in the Midwest at that time the Ku Klux Klan imposed itself, burning crosses. Yet many decent people still regarded the white-robed organization as a harmless band of superpatriots who feared, among other things, domination of the United States by the Pope in Rome.

Truman considered joining. There are conflicting stories of what happened next. One is that the Klan maintained that Harry's maternal grandfather, Solomon Young, was Jewish and threatened exposure unless Truman went along. Bess advised extreme caution about affiliation with such a group. Another is that Harry desperately wanted the Klan's political support and paid the $10 initiation fee. The Klan insisted that Harry pledge that he wouldn't give county jobs to Catholics. Again Bess urged prudence.

The Klan decided to oppose Truman and sent him a batch of letters that warned, "Keep your fool mouth shut or else . . ." He didn't. He was in those days launching his "Give 'em hell" style, and despite his outspokenness he was elected. "Harry was terrible when delivering a prepared speech," Miss Noland said. "But when it was off the cuff, everybody sat up and took notice. I always thought it was

Bess who realized it first. Though she was afraid that he'd be carried away and say something embarrassing."

Truman remembered that first victory well. "The next morning," he recalled, "Bess asked me, 'And what does Judge Truman want for breakfast?' I answered, 'Two eggs, please, judge's wife.' We both laughed. I must admit we liked the sound of the new label."

Bess and Harry may have been impressed with the title. Mrs. Wallace was not. "Mr. Truman isn't a real judge!" she said haughtily. "He can't even marry anybody or sentence a robber caught in the act."

Judge Truman was sworn into office in January, 1923. There was a great deal he planned to accomplish during the next two years. He discussed his anticipated course of action with his wife—a habit he was to follow the remainder of his life: "I never make a decision unless Bess is in on it."

She felt Jackson County's traffic system should be improved. Together they rode over every inch of the muddy roads, which were in such bad shape they had to put bags of cement in the rear of the car to keep themselves from being tossed through the windshield.

During one of their road-inspection trips, the Truman car suffered a blowout. Miraculously, Harry avoided a head-on collision with a large coal truck. He managed to get his ailing car to the side of the road, where he proceeded to change the tire.

Dr. Plunkett, the minister of the Independence Trinity Episcopal Church, drove by as Bess was wheeling the spare over to her husband. The clergyman stopped and offered his assistance. Harry replied that everything was under control and that Bess was giving him all the help he needed. The minister drove off. The following Sunday his sermon revolved around Ecclesiasticus 26:1—*"Happy is the husband of a good wife."*

Once when Bess accompanied Harry to the Jackson County Old Folks Home, an eighty-year-old woman timidly approached her. "Dearie," she whispered, "things may look shipshape when you're here, but the minute you leave they will go right back to being horrible!" Then she proceeded to list the deplorable conditions.

On the ride home Truman decided that a thorough investigation should be launched. It led to a complete overhaul of the Old Folks Home, and several years later the institution was singled out as a model for the entire state.

"Whenever Bess felt changes should be made, she would offer her recommendations to Harry," said Charlie Ross, his press secretary. "Always she would do it in her dignified, ladylike manner. Invariably, he'd act on them. She was the one who thought public officials should have backgrounds in law. He enrolled in the Kansas City Law School and attended several nights a week. He was a good student."

By the end of Truman's term, the court was so improved that the Kansas City *Star,* a Republican newspaper that usually was hostile to anyone remotely linked to Pendergast, published an extremely laudatory editorial:

> The present [Pendergast] court is busy paying off the debt. It paid off more than $600,000 last year. It has improved the roads. It has money in the treasury. That is the difference between county courts. The men who did this, Judge McElroy and Judge Truman, are up for renomination. Tuesday the Democratic voters in Jackson County will show whether they are interested enough in good service to renominate the men who are responsible for this remarkable showing.

Despite the *Star*'s flattering story, Harry was defeated. "The Klan worked overtime to beat him," Mrs. Haukenberry said. It was the only defeat Harry ever suffered. To complicate matters, Margaret had arrived some months earlier.

"Harry was overjoyed when he learned he was going to

become a father," said Ethel Noland. "However, the truth
is that he was more than a little scared. He was so stirred up
you'd think no one had ever been pregnant before. Bess, on
the other hand, was her normal self—dignified and never let
on she had a moment of discomfort."

A neighbor remembers her mother telling her about
Truman's deep concern. "One night she was having dinner
with them," the woman said. "All the guests were having
coffee and pie topped with whipped cream. Mr. Truman
snatched the coffee and dessert away from his wife. Instead,
he substituted a glass of milk.

"'That's much better for your condition!' he lectured.
When she finished, he escorted her to the parlor—practically carried her. And it was only her second month!"

The forty-year-old father dropped out of night law school
and desperately looked for work. "I spent a long time
thinking and trying to make some bread and butter for my
sweetheart and our small daughter," he said.

Bess's family offered to help them, but he was firmly
opposed. He finally got a job selling memberships in the
Kansas City Automobile Club. He was a good salesman,
and during one campaign he sold fifteen hundred memberships. Soon he was earning $5000 a year. Out of his earnings
the Trumans managed to make regular payments on the
obligations left over from the ill-fated business venture that
Bess's mother referred to as Mr. Truman's foolish error.

Although Harry could now adequately provide for his
wife and daughter, Bess sensed that her husband wasn't
happy as a salesman. "Not that he ever complains," she told
a friend. "But sometimes he gets up during the night and
just stares."

When they learned that a tiny bank near Independence
was for sale, they became very interested. For $30,000 the
Security Bank of Englewood could be purchased outright.
The most attractive feature of the deal was that it didn't
require any down payment, as the chief stockholder was
willing to take the $30,000 in notes.

With his wife's approval, Harry decided to become a banker. Just after the final papers were signed, a large number of fraudulent entries were discovered in the bank's bookkeeping. "That was the moment Bess persuaded Harry to make a fast exit," Miss Noland recalled. "It was in the nick of time—a short time later the bank failed!"

Another election was coming up that year, and the Trumans had decided that Harry should try to get back into politics. The office they had in mind was that of county collector. Salary: $25,000 a year. Boss Pendergast, when he was consulted, vetoed the idea and instead offered Truman the nomination for presiding judge of the county court. Salary: $6000.

"Once more they had a lengthy conference," said Vaughan. "They discussed the pros and cons. Bess was never happy in politics, but she was practical."

During the campaign a great many politicians visited the Delaware Street house. Mrs. Wallace wasn't pleased about the guests and considered them unwelcome intruders and "a bunch of coarse louts." She was delighted at what happened when one ward heeler picked up little Margaret and tried to kiss her. The frightened youngster pinched his bulbous nose as hard as she could, and he screamed in pain. Bess's mother said loudly, "Serves the old fool right!"

This time the Klan didn't interfere and Harry won the election. The first order of business was parceling out nine hundred jobs. Harry had always been a loyal organization man, and he reluctantly agreed that the jobs should go to Pendergast faithfuls. When the matter was taken care of to the political boss's satisfaction, Pendergast moved on to state and national affairs and left Harry pretty much alone. Presiding Judge Truman promptly enforced a stricter contractor inspection to determine competence. He drastically curbed expense accounts and reorganized the county's borrowing procedure.

In 1930 he was reelected to the same office. During his two four-year terms, Bess liked to boast that he also pushed through the building of miles of good country roads, built a badly needed waterworks, several modern playgrounds, a hospital for the aged and a new four-million-dollar courthouse. She urged Harry to make known his accomplishments and helped him prepare a booklet: *Results of County Planning—Jackson County.* It resulted in Truman being chosen as president of the Greater Kansas City Planning Association and as a director of the National Conference of City Planning. He had a statewide reputation, and it was a good one.

"It was while he was presiding judge that the attempted kidnapping occurred," said Ethel Noland. "Harry, Bess and Margaret were always very close. What affected one, affected all. They weren't called the three musketeers for nothing. It's only natural that a family would be terribly upset by a kidnapping threat. But for the Trumans it was a shock beyond belief when Margaret was the intended victim."

One day a heavyset man appeared at the school Margaret was attending and said that Judge Truman had sent him, "to pick up Mary." Fortunately the teacher was alert. Although the youngster had been christened Mary Margaret, she was always called by her middle name. The instructor said she would get the child, but instead she quickly phoned Truman, who immediately called the police. However, the mysterious stranger was gone when they arrived. After that scare Bess drove Margaret to school and called for her long before her first-grade class was dismissed. "I'm taking no chances," she told neighbors.

Soon after the kidnapping alarm, life for the Trumans returned to being calm and conventional. On Sundays they visited Harry's mother and sister in nearby Grandview. He joined the prestigious Kansas City Athletic Club. He learned to swim while keeping his head out of the water, so he could wear his glasses. "That way I'll know where the shallow end is," he explained.

He grew a mustache, but Bess felt it made him look less distinguished. Then he attempted a beard but gave it up because she insisted that the hair on the right side of his face grew upward and on the left side went down.

As the second term of his county judgeship neared its end, he and Bess began to think of the next step, since it wasn't customary for a presiding judge to serve more than eight years. It was widely rumored that several previous Jackson County jurists had left office with hundreds of thousands of illegally acquired dollars. It was almost expected of them. But it was never said of Harry. The Trumans were almost broke. They didn't even have enough money to make a payment on the $8,944 debt that was still owed on the ill-fated haberdashery project. And no jobs were in sight. Pendergast didn't make any overtures. It seemed that fifty-year-old Truman's political career had reached a dead end. The machine had already named the candidates for county collector and congressman. Sadly, Bess told Ethel Noland, "Harry feels what's in store for him is retirement in some very minor county office."

She and her husband weren't prepared for the Pendergast offer of support for him as U.S. senator. Although Harry was the boss's fourth choice, they wonderingly accepted.

VI HER HUSBAND, THE SENATOR FROM PENDERGAST

AGAIN WITH MACHINE support Harry was victorious, with a plurality of 262,000 votes. The Trumans were going to Washington.

While the junior senator-elect looked for a place to live, Mrs. Truman and Margaret, now ten, were left temporarily behind. At a session of the Independence Bridge Club, Bess was asked, "Aren't you worried about your husband running around loose among all those pretty government secretaries?"

"No," she replied simply. "Three no trump."

"Those two never had the slightest doubts about each other," said Ethel Noland. "Bess was sure that he was busy searching for an apartment and that was that. It had to have some outside play area, as she had doubts about raising a child in Washington."

Truman looked over the city where he thought he'd remain for the next six years. He told some constituents from Missouri, "My trouble is that I probably won't find a place to live. You see, I have to live on my salary [at the time senators earned $10,000 a year] and a cubbyhole rents for $150 a month. The ones that are fit to live in run from $250 to $500 a month, and although it's hard to believe there are some saphead senators who pay $1500 a month for their apartments. . . . I am undoubtedly the poorest senator financially in Washington."

"Harry finally located a small furnished four-room apartment for $125 a month just off Connecticut Avenue," said John Snyder, secretary of the treasury in Truman's cabinet and perhaps the closest family intimate. "The only extravagance was the rental of a piano for Margaret. He sent for his family."

One of the first things that Bess saw in the nation's capital was a copy of an article titled: "The Senator from Pendergast." It pictured Truman as an obscure, near-bankrupt haberdasher who had gone to the political boss to ask for the county collectorship and had received the Senate seat as a consolation prize.

Soon after reading that story Bess had further demonstrations of her husband's unpopularity in the Capitol. It was a long-standing Washington custom that on Thursday afternoons Senate wives poured tea for the mates of new members. Mrs. Truman attended several of these receptions. She found some of the women openly hostile to and contemptuous of the wife of "Pendergast's errand boy."

"When she reported it, he was furious," said Victor Messall, Harry's chief congressional aide, "and wanted to strike back. It was Mrs. Truman who persuaded him to ignore the gossip. She also counseled him to refrain from using such outrageous epithets as 'saphead senators.' It was probably difficult going but he listened to her, as he was determined to be a good legislator. He'd take reams of work home. Sometimes he'd get so tired that he'd fall asleep and his wife would have to wake him to go to bed."

Mary Schindler, who worked in the Congressional Library, also spoke of Truman's fervency. "He'd spend hours in the stalls," she recalled. "Most of the other senators used messengers. Not him. He'd come in with a long list of books he wished to see. Some hadn't been checked out in ten years. I was very impressed and asked him where he got it. 'The boss,' he answered. He didn't mean Pendergast but Mrs. Truman."

The cramped four-room apartment was quite a change for Bess, who had lived all her life in much more luxurious quarters. "She never complained," said Vaughan. "She did the cooking, the washing and most of the cleaning. Harry would remark that she was a fine gourmet cook. But I wondered how he knew since he was strictly a steak-and-potatoes man."

Paul Kupferman, part-owner of a small grocery store Bess frequented, recalled, "That apartment was always spotless. Every time I made a delivery I'd remark, 'It's so clean you could eat off the floor.' It got to be a regular joke as Mrs. Truman would always reply, 'Thank you for the compliment. But if you don't mind I'd rather eat at the table.' She'd rarely speak of anything personal. The only time I remember she did was once we had a special on macaroni—I believe it was three packages for 39 cents. She bought six. As I put them in a bag, she said, 'They'll probably complain. However, that's one way of keeping the wolf from the door.' She was a careful shopper."

He recalled another characteristic. "When the store was busy she'd patiently—almost humbly—wait her turn. She'd give it up if she felt someone else was more deserving. Once it was an old man who had to use two canes to walk. After he left she remarked, 'I guess I can afford standing more than he can.' Despite the fact that I'd heard she had trouble with one of her knees and was always in pain when she stood a long time. Not once did she take advantage of being a senator's wife. She's a very decent human being."

Rose Zarwitz, an employee in a neighborhood cleaning

store, endorsed Kupferman's opinion. "I didn't even know that Mrs. Truman was married to a senator," she said. "It was only when I saw his picture in the paper that I found out. She was such a plain person—never acted fancy. A real *mensch*.* She'd come in the shop with a smile on her face and ask me how I was. Margaret was also like that. I'm sure Mrs. Truman taught her that way. Those two were as close as fishballs in a vacuum jar. You never saw one without the other. I used to remark to Mr. Tash, my brother-in-law, 'There goes a good mother!'"

Margaret was enrolled in Gunston Hall, a small private school for young ladies that was run in the old Southern tradition. Each morning Bess drove her daughter to classes and promptly called for her when school let out. At first they were both lonely for Independence, where the name Truman was extremely popular. It wasn't so in Washington. Most of the press agreed with a radio commentator who said, "Truman's only passing through . . . a strawman . . . a Pendergast puppet!"

So Bess and Margaret did what all tourists do in the nation's capital—they went sightseeing. They visited the Smithsonian Institution, the Washington Monument, the Lincoln Memorial, Mount Vernon, the Tomb of the Unknown Soldier, Lee's mansion. "They also did some rubbernecking in the White House," said Messall. "Mrs. Truman and Margaret stood in line to catch a glimpse of some of the rooms that were open to the public. When they got out, Margaret told her mother that it had been a waste of time. I think Mrs. Truman agreed."

Mother and daughter developed a firm friendship. "It was during those times I think we really got to know each other well," Margaret once told anthropologist Margaret Mead.†

---

* A Yiddish expression: "A very decent person."
† Some years ago I brought Margaret Truman Daniel and Margaret Mead together for a joint interview. The results of that meeting appeared in *Redbook* magazine.

"I learned that Mother is a warmhearted, kind lady of tremendous character. She would constantly make me laugh with her ever-present merry wit. She's undoubtedly the least understood member of our family. Without her, my father and I would have been utterly lost. . . . She's the secret of our success. . . . I won't say that everything always went along smoothly. I did need some disciplining and she was the one to do it. Used her hands or a brush. My father never spanked me."

When mother and daughter didn't go sightseeing, they would window shop and occasionally visit an old-fashioned ice-cream parlor on Connecticut Avenue that made wonderful sodas and sundaes. Margaret wanted to go more often, but Bess felt it was too expensive.

"I wouldn't call her a tightwad," said Miss Noland. "But she was pretty conservative about money. Margaret got 25 cents a week allowance. She was regularly running short and then Harry would slip her some extra change. Bess protested. 'Harry,' she'd scold. 'How can I ever teach this child the value of money without your cooperation?'"

During that first year Mrs. Roosevelt invited Margaret, along with the children of other senators, to a lavish dancing party at the White House. Bess declined and sent Eleanor a respectful but firm note, explaining that Margaret was only eleven years old and not yet ready for dancing parties.

"I believe Mrs. Truman was a bit sorry she had to refuse," Messall said. "It would have given her a chance to see Mrs. Roosevelt, whom she greatly admired. Once Mrs. Truman accidentally spilled ink on an autographed photograph of the First Lady. It was ruined. She was overjoyed when I managed to get her another one."

In addition to taking care of the house and shepherding Margaret around Washington, Bess worked in her husband's Senate office as a $4500 assistant. One of her major tasks was to handle appeals from people back home. One request came from Truman's birthplace in Lamar, Missouri.

The writer had been refused a job in the local post office and cautioned Harry "not to get too big for your britches!" Bess turned over the letter to her husband with a rough sketch she drew of a man wearing baggy trousers and a very high hat. Underneath the drawing she added a caption: "A bad case of Potomac fever!"

That she held a job in her husband's office was eventually made public. She and Harry received a lot of flak. "The faultfinders," said Messall, "didn't realize that Mrs. Truman did most of her work at home—no union hours for her. That lady worked long and hard."

Even the Pendergast baiter, Republican Roy Roberts, managing editor of the Kansas City *Star,* similarly defended her. "She earned every penny," he said vehemently.

Despite the steady stream of criticism, the Trumans were celebrities to their neighbors. Barbara Heiler, a former history professor at the University of Chicago, spoke fondly of them. "I was thrilled to live in the same house," she said. "Mrs. Truman would greet me warmly when we'd meet in the hallway. The newspapers were so wrong when they called her grim-faced. Once you got to know her she was anything but that. Due to their sharp interest in history, I knew them rather well. Once I mentioned that I was driving to the Midwest to see my aunt in Omaha. Mrs. Truman gave me the names of people I should visit along the way. I did. I had never met them, but they treated me as if I were a long-lost cousin. I discovered the reason. She had written to them and strongly requested that they be cordial. She was always like that. It seemed that the only thing that would cause her to frown was when someone was unkind to her husband or daughter."

Miss Heiler spoke of another incident that revealed Bess's humaneness. "One time a pipe burst in the hallway," she recalled. "The entire place was suddenly filled with water. While the janitor tried to repair the leak, several of the tenants—chiefly Mrs. Truman—emptied the water. I know it was hard work, as I bailed alongside her. Throughout it all she never lost her sense of humor. As she emptied one bucket she remarked, 'This should bring my waist down. As a matter of fact it's so good for me that I think I'll bust another pipe.'"

During Harry's first term, Pathé News sent a crew to his office to film some of his daily activities. They wasted a great deal of footage because of his ineptness as an actor. "Speak up!" the director shouted. Finally, in desperation, the frustrated man bit the stem of his eyeglasses and then moaned, "An FDR he isn't!"

Whereupon Bess, who had witnessed the debacle, said, "You are quite right. He's HST! And proud of it!"

Messall said, "I'll always remember the tender and grateful look Truman gave her. And the one she gave him in return."

VII HER HUSBAND, THE SENATOR'S SENATOR

BESS WAS SOCIALLY accepted by the other congressional wives at the same time that Harry was admitted to the "club."* The Trumans had survived observation, faithfully served their apprenticeships and had qualified. Suddenly invitations from the official Washington circuit covered Harry's desk and jammed the tiny mailbox in their apartment house.

Bess's head was not turned. Holding a gilt-edged invitation in one hand, she would say, "Do you think we can afford a sitter for Margaret? We're pretty short this month."

*There is no club. Not, that is, as a formal organization. Nevertheless, it is one of the world's most exclusive fellowships. This clannish Upper House inner circle has frozen out many well-known senators. Explained John Nance Garner, FDR's two-term vice-president, "Those fellows didn't fit. Harry did." Probable definition of fitness: hard-nosed political know-how covered by a veneer of *bonhomie*. At social events, which deceive no one as to their purpose, members wheel, deal and exchange information.

The Trumans chose to attend the less formal parties. Following one, Mrs. Burton K. Wheeler, wife of the Republican senator from Montana, remarked, "My husband says, 'Harry Truman is now one of the boys.' Usually a wife is accepted on her husband's merits, but the truth is Bess was 'in' before he was. She was careful not to let him know it. She wouldn't have dreamed of going it alone without him, even though she might have successfully maneuvered to his advantage in our women's circle. That's not the way she does things."

Veteran civil rights attorney Morris Ernst said, "What tipped the scales was when Truman was made vice-chairman of the Senate Committee on Interstate Commerce, which was then conducting hearings on railroad finances. It brought him to the attention of Supreme Court Justice Louis Brandeis. Many of Harry's fellow senators didn't approve of Brandeis, a liberal dissenter, who denounced 'the curse of bigness,' but they greatly respected his perception. If he accepted Truman, that was good enough for them.

"The justice once told me that he saw Harry as 'shrewd, honest, capable, a man who takes the long view.' From then on Harry was approved.

Brandeis summoned Truman to his California Street apartment and discovered that despite their very different backgrounds (Louis Dembitz Brandeis was Jewish, son of immigrants, a graduate of Harvard Law School, and an Easterner), they shared similar views: Monopolies were generally bad. Where they were evident they should be attacked. When it was necessary, they should be carefully watched.

Harry was invited back again and again. Bess encouraged the meetings and was pleased when her husband told her, "The old man backs me in a corner and pays no attention to anyone else while he talks transportation to me."

The Supreme Court justice chuckled at a speech Truman delivered on the floor of the Senate:

> The first railroad robbery was committed on the Rock Island back in 1873 just east of Council Bluffs, Iowa. The man who committed that robbery used a gun and a horse, and got up early in the morning. He and his gang took a chance on being killed and eventually most were. The loot was $3,000. That railroad robber's name was Jesse James. . . . About thirty years after the Council Bluff's holdup, the Rock Island went through a looting by some gentlemen known as the 'Tin Plate Millionaires.' They used no guns, but they ruined the railroad and got away with $70,000,000 or more. They did it by means of holding companies. Senators can see what pikers Mr. James and his crowd were alongside some real artists.

Ernst said that Bess had suggested the theme. "She didn't give him the exact words but said that it was her idea that he liken the theft to Jesse James."

Truman was often called a two-fisted drinker. Close friends dispute this. They insisted that he and Bess were prudent, defensive drinkers. Bourbon was their favorite. "She would rarely take more than one," a White House aide said. "The President liked to give the impression that he was a stiff, manly boozer. Yet he would often stretch each drink out for as long as possible." A few days after the railroad speech, the Trumans attended a large Washington cocktail party. A very conservative former congressman approached Harry and reprimanded him for using the safety of the Senate floor to compare transportation officials to notorious highwaymen. Truman, who was eating hors d'oeuvres, suddenly pretended his fork was a gun and pointed it at the startled guest. "Your money or your life!" he said jokingly.

At which point Bess, as always cautious in public, whispered, "Harry, your dignity, please! Save your weapons for the Senate floor!" The incident became a twenty-four-hour Washington gossip item. Several days later the same ex-Congressman was indicted for fraud.

"How did your husband know?" Bess was asked.

She smiled, sighed, shook her head. "Antenna," she said. "He can always tell the good guys from the bad."

On one of the return trips Harry went through a full stop sign at a key intersection in Hagerstown, Maryland. Another car plowed into him, causing the Truman vehicle to strike a lamp post. "Part of it fell down on the car and gave Bess an awful jolt," Truman said. "Her neck has never been quite right since." He suffered a minor cut on his forehead. Margaret, who was sitting in the back, was pulled out of a window, frightened but uninjured. She escaped with a bad scare. The car, completely demolished, was towed to a scrap heap.

Every summer Truman spent two weeks in the army reserve. He was now a colonel in command of a regiment. Snyder, who had also retained his reserve commission, recalled, "After hours we'd sit around and gab. Harry always turned the conversation around to something Bess or Margaret did. I've never seen such a family man. Once we were invited by the man who published *Cap'n Billy's Whiz Bang* to his place in Minnesota. It was a beautiful summer home and each time we'd spot some lovely view, tree, flower, or a bird, Harry would remark, 'If Bess and Margaret could only see this.' Here he was a full-fledged colonel and a U.S. senator who was lost without his wife and daughter!"

While Truman was away on military duty, Bess did some much-needed discarding. "With Harry out of the house," she told her Independence Bridge Club, "I can throw out some of the junk we've accumulated. That is, if it's okay to do spring cleaning in August? Fortunately, the apartments we've lived in in Washington have always been too small to clutter up. Also, Harry is so busy there that he hasn't any time to do any collecting."

She granted one of her rare interviews to a Kansas City reporter. "You can guess," she said, "that it is very different from my life in Independence. The lonesomeness that one feels in that first introduction in Washington fades, however. One finds new friends, scores of them. How satisfying after a while to see their smiling faces at some formal occasion. I had rather feared, as any Midwestern woman might, the coldness of an Eastern city. Rather I found Washington replete with a hospitality where the administrative tangles are a distinct part of the conversation in the Congressional Club where I belong. I found the Senate women only too glad to talk of household matters and family questions, as women will in any part of the world."

As the Trumans were at last learning to enjoy Washington, Roosevelt sent word that he didn't think Harry could possibly win renomination to the Senate. Instead, he offered to appoint him to the Interstate Commerce Commission. The President was obviously motivated by Pendergast's recent indictment for income tax evasion. (The political boss was found guilty. He was sentenced to fifteen months in Leavenworth and fined $10,000. He agreed to pay the government $434,000 in back taxes.)

"Truman stormed out of his Senate office," Messall recalled. "He said he was heading home 'where I'm understood.' The next day he sent FDR a message that he would run if he only got one vote—his own! When Mrs. Truman heard about it, she said, 'Harry has made a slight error. He can count on another sure vote—mine!'"

Ethel Noland said, "Bess was really het up about that

primary. She felt it was the most vicious she had ever seen. That if all the mud slung could be set in piles, they would cover the entire state of Missouri.''

Regardless of all the dirty fighting, Bess strongly counseled her husband to avoid using similar tactics against his two opponents, Missouri Governor Lloyd Stark, who was the owner of extensive orchards where the famous hybrid apple called Stark's Delicious first appeared, and District Attorney Maurice Milligan, the Pendergast prosecutor—both of whom yearned to replace Harry on the Democratic ticket.

Once again the Trumans began vigorous, old-style campaigning in the boondocks. They visited seventy-five counties during a scorching July and August. If there was a clam bake or picnic, they made appearances. Bess didn't say much, but when the time came for her husband to speak, she would judiciously nod her head and discreetly beam. She was responsible for some of his best lines: "Any farmer who is dang fool enough to vote for another farmer who's losing money farming ought to have his head examined!" That took care of Stark. "And any farmer who's dang fool enough to vote for a lawyer who never sees a farm ought to have his head examined twice!" That took care of Milligan, a city slicker.

She was pleased to find that his speeches always brought loud cheers, although she had expected him to present them in a somewhat more dignified fashion. Like a proud grandma, she frowned on Harry's salty language. A story that Truman liked to tell dealt with a speech he delivered at a Kansas City Grange Convention. Bess and a friend were in the audience and heard him say to the Grangers, "I grew up on a farm, and one thing I'm sure about is that farming means manure, manure and more manure."

Down in the auditorium Bess's companion whispered to her, "Why on earth can't you get Harry to use a more genteel word?"

To which Bess replied, "Good Lord, Helen, it's taken me years to get him to use 'manure'!"

Down-to-earth behavior seems to have run in the Truman family. During the campaign, Harry's mother attended a meeting in Sedalia, Missouri, and when Stark's name was mentioned, the eighty-eight-year-old-woman booed loudly. Bess, who had always been on cordial terms with her mother-in-law, turned and patted her cheek. A man sitting directly behind them heard her say, "Mother Truman, that's exactly how I feel. He's a completely incompetent man. Even the worms in his apples have worms."

The Trumans worked hard, but it looked as though the election odds were just too high to surmount. The night of the primary, Harry went to bed at midnight a very tired and discouraged candidate. He was eleven thousand votes behind, and his top supporters were ready to concede. Bess vetoed the idea. "It wasn't that she was optimistic," Messall said. "She simply felt it was too early."

At 3:30 A.M. the phone rang. Bess answered it. "This is Dave Bernstein," a voice at the other end said. "I'd like to congratulate the wife of the senator from Missouri."

"I don't think that's very funny," she replied as she slammed down the receiver. A few seconds later she realized that Dave Bernstein was their campaign manager in St. Louis. She promptly called him back. Yes, it was true. Harry was running ahead. The desperate beating of the bushes had paid off in a very narrow victory. Bess later described the triumph as being so thin it would make Slim Summerville (a Hollywood character who was popular in the thirties. One reviewer wrote, "Summerville is so skinny he could slip through a keyhole carrying a knapsack.") seem fat by comparison. When the final votes were counted, Truman had received 262,552, Stark—254,585, Milligan—125,024.

"The election in November was a shoo-in," Messall said. "Truman, like all those who had been faithful to the

administration, was victorious. He carried the state easily
and now was a senator without the aid of Pendergast, who
was in jail."

Harry returned to Washington the following day. "When
he walked out on the floor, all the senators—Democrats
and Republicans—up and applauded," Bess said proudly.
"I think that was the moment Harry really felt that he was
one of them. Up until then he had been awed by their
sophisticated backgrounds. Most had graduated from college. They were ex-governors, high executives—things like
that. But now he, too, belonged."

"The Trumans didn't have to spend their leisure time
sightseeing anymore," said Jane Lingo, one of Margaret's
very close companions. "They made many lifelong friends
in Washington. Once you got to know the Trumans, you
instinctively took to them." Jane, who had been Margaret's
classmate, recalled, "Mrs. Truman would pick her up and
I'd also pile in the car. I know that Mrs. Truman was a good
deal older than us, but she fitted right in. It wasn't that she
was being deliberately pushy or anything like that. It was
because she was always so lighthearted and cheerful—it was
catching!

"The three of us would chatter away. Insignificant things
like songs and actors. A favorite tune of hers was 'Clear
Blue Water.' She'd hum it and then apologize for her voice.
The actors she particularly liked were Clark Gable, Bing
Crosby and Bob Hope. She loved the *Road* pictures. So did
Mr. Truman. Sometimes I'd go to the movies with the
entire family. Margaret's mother and father weren't very
demonstrative in public, but as soon as the lights dimmed,
they held hands. They continued that practice right into the
White House theater. There was never any question of how
they felt about each other."

Another Washington friend that Bess often saw was Mrs.
Fred Vinson, wife of the director of the Office of War
Mobilization and Reconversion. When Truman became

President, he appointed Vinson secretary of the treasury and later chief justice of the Supreme Court. One day as the two women were having tea, Margaret wandered by. "She looks so much like her father," said Mrs. Vinson. "No one can say she's the iceman's daughter," Bess howled.

One Sunday afternoon during a ride to Grandview, Harry remarked that the recently widowed wife of a Southern senator might be appointed to fill out her late husband's unexpired term. He indicated he would be happy if the same thing happened if he suddenly died. The following day Truman told Senator Alben Barkley of Kentucky and Senator Tom Connally of Texas about Bess's reaction. "She sure blew her top," he said. "I've never seen her so mad. She burst out, 'Harry, if you dare to die I promise I'll never speak to you! And you know I mean it! Now stop that foolish kind of talk!'"

Barkley, who was majority leader of the Senate, said, "She's right. We need you right here. The work you're doing is very necessary." Later he told Connally, "Mark my words, one day soon that Truman will develop into being a senators' senator."

Hugh Fulton, a brilliant young government attorney, also realized Truman's potential when he left a high-ranking Justice Department position to switch to the newly formed Special Committee to Investigate the National Defense Program, later shortened to the chairman's name: the Truman Committee.

"I could tell it was going to be important," Fulton said. "So could Truman's wife. As a matter of fact, in some ways it was her idea. They were sitting around having one of their usual evening talk sessions when Harry told her about the staggering sum the government was losing in defense at Fort Leonard Wood in Rolla, Missouri. He said that he heard contractors were padding payrolls and taking kickbacks from workers, charging for unnecessary work and work not done.

"Harry always gave her a good deal of credit for what happened next. 'She told me to do some of my own checking. Packed my bags and sent me on my way to do some firsthand looking. . . . The trip was an eye opener, and I came back to Washington convinced that something had to be done fast.'"

The result was a sweeping investigation of all defense contracts. The Truman Committee saved the country millions of dollars by curbing waste and discouraging graft. Harry's exhaustive probing meant constant traveling, and toward the end of 1941 he was in the Midwest. On Saturday night of December 6, he called Bess from a small hotel in Columbia, Missouri. He sounded very weary and admitted that he had had an extremely grueling week. She ordered him to spend the next day in bed. Ordinarily he would have balked at such a suggestion. This time he docilely agreed. His last words were that if all went well he could meet her in Independence, where the family could all share Christmas.

The following afternoon Bess was busy writing letters. Margaret was home nursing a cold and listening to a concert on the radio. Suddenly a voice interrupted the music with an announcement that the Japanese had attacked Pearl Harbor. Margaret thought Pearl Harbor was somewhere in China and couldn't understand the intrusion. Irritably she told her mother about it. Bess, who isn't easily flustered, tripped as she rushed to the phone to call Harry. He had taken her advice and was half-asleep when he answered. She relayed the news and cautioned him, "Be careful."

He managed to get a small private plane to fly him to St. Louis, where he boarded a night flight to Washington. He arrived just in time to vote aye for the United States declaring war.

A few weeks later Bess and Harry had one of their rare disputes. Truman, who was still a colonel in the reserve, saw many of his friends returning to active status. He also wanted to join up. She tried to convince him that he was badly needed on the home front. He continued to plead. Finally she gave in. With her approval he called on General George Marshall to secure his permission to join the regular army.

Marshall looked at the gray-haired senator. "How old are you?" he asked.

"Fifty-six."

"You're too damned old! Stay in the Senate where you're needed!"

For the next hour Harry sulked. Then Bess, who now spent most of her time in his Senate office, asked him a question about war preparedness. She smiled and saluted him. He grinned and returned the salute. Soon Truman was back at work, searching out careless spending and corruption.

"Father always was busy," Margaret recalled. "He looked exhausted and grave. My mother always looked worried."

One of the few times they appeared relaxed was on June 2, 1942, Margaret's graduation from Gunston Hall. They were delighted when their daughter received the English prize as well as the Spanish award. Harry delivered the commencement address and proudly told the audience that he was glad that Margaret took after her mother in those subjects. Bess's face turned crimson.

That summer the family returned to Independence. Harry spent little time there, as he had to attend dozens of hearings in Washington or inspect ordnance plants in California or Texas. At one point the journeys became so frequent that Bess told Ethel Noland, "I feel like the wife of a traveling salesman."

A letter Truman wrote indicated that he, too, was upset. "Get up at 5:30, drink tomato juice and milk, go to work, eat some toast and orange juice and work some more, maybe have a committee fight, go to bed at midnight and start over."

Normally, Harry managed to conceal his frustration. However, it became very visible when his close friend Harry Vaughan talked his way into being put on active duty. "That really threw him," Bess said. It helped a little when she showed him a clipping from *The New York Times* that indicated the Truman Committee was making "a decisive contribution to the prosecution of the war."

The investigation had made Harry a minor national figure. More favorable stories about him began appearing. Bess was particularly pleased when *Reader's Digest* ran one called "Billion-Dollar Watchdog." The magazine was a favorite in Independence. She was thrilled when several members of her bridge club called to say how much they had enjoyed it. When Harry's picture appeared on the cover of *Time,* Bess said, "Not even Clare Boothe Luce can stop him now." Coolly, quietly, she was preparing for him to be considered as a candidate for Vice-President.

VIII SECOND LADY OF THE LAND

"IF THE TRUTH be known," said Ethel Noland, "Bess did and didn't want to be Mrs. Vice-President. She really had mixed feelings. She was humanly tempted by the second highest rank and honor in the country, but she worried lest the constant public glare might prove to be unfair to twenty-year-old Margaret, who at the time was a young college student. Bess had seen what high-powered limelight had done to the Roosevelt children. Nevertheless, as always, she was a dutiful wife and wanted the best for her husband."

Truman, aware of his wife's ambivalence, had tangled sentiments about being the candidate to unseat Henry Wallace, FDR's third term Vice-President, a fellow Midwesterner and farmer he had always admired.* On the

---

*The decision of Roosevelt and his close advisers to dump the incumbent Vice-President still makes a good guessing game. The best supposition is that FDR, with an eye on postwar politics, felt that organized labor, which backed Wallace, was in the bag, Wallace or no Wallace, and that the political machines, which Truman had just proved he could control were not.

afternoon of the balloting, Roosevelt asked party chief
Robert Hannegan, "Bob, have you got that fellow Truman
lined up yet?"

"No," said Hannegan. "He is a contrary Missouri mule."

"Well, you tell him," said the President, "if he wants to
break up the Democratic Party in the middle of a war, that's
his responsibility!"

Only then, goes the quasi-authoritative account, did
Harry agree to run. "Well, if that is the situation, I'll have
to say yes," was his crusty reply. "But why the hell didn't he
put it that way in the first place?"

Jonathan Daniels, a Roosevelt aide who assisted Truman
during the transition period, had some other thoughts. "I
come now in my old age to a wry grin about Harry
Truman," Daniels said. "He seemed then no more than an
ordinary, simple, straightforward country citizen. I missed,
in my 1950 biography of Truman, what seems plain to me
now. I feel certain that he played the role of the reluctant
candidate with the skill of the maestro. No man ever played
hard to get with more conviction than Harry Truman."

Daniels, a devoted Truman admirer, added, "Somebody
real bright wrote the scenario of just how it should be done.
And that somebody may well have been his wife."

Bess came as near to elation in public as she ever showed
when she heard her husband's name placed in nomination
by Bennet Clark, the senior senator from Missouri. She
smiled, then her mouth tightened to show discomfort as she
spotted Mrs. Henry Wallace in Chicago's Convention Hall.
She liked the Vice-President's wife, whose daughter Jean
was a friend of Margaret's. She didn't speak much during
the voting. However, when Maryland's Governor
O'Connor swung his state's eighteen votes to Harry, she
again smiled slightly. "She knew it was the beginning of the
end for Wallace," said Mrs. India Edwards, who later was
appointed vice-chairwoman of the Democratic National
Committee. "Bess has always been a shrewd politician."

Truman's acceptance speech was one of the shortest ever delivered. The brevity was advised by Bess. "She felt most of them were far too verbose and sounded like so many long-winded funeral orations," said Snyder.

This one certainly wasn't long-winded—it consisted of 91 words:

> You don't know how very much I appreciate the very great honor which has come to the state of Missouri. It is also a great responsibility which I am perfectly willing to assume.
>
> Nine years and five months ago I came to the Senate. I expect to continue the efforts I have made there to help shorten the war and win the peace under the great leader, Franklin D. Roosevelt.
>
> I don't know what else I can say except that I accept this great honor with all humility.
>
> I thank you.

"Bess may not have had a very broad smile," said Edwin Pauley, treasurer of the Democratic National Committee, "but she certainly looked proud. And why not? Bess Truman is a realist. She knew she would shortly be not only the wife of the Vice-President but very soon the wife of the President. Everyone close to Roosevelt knew that he was a dying man and that we hadn't just voted for Vice-President but President!" *

As soon as Harry finished, while the audience still stamped and cheered, he fought his way off the platform

---

*Some years later I wrote an article for *Reader's Digest* with Admiral Ross McIntyre, FDR's personal physician. Dr. McIntyre told me, "No, it wasn't apparent that he might well have to bow out from the very vigorous role of conducting the arduous role of continuing in office. However, there lurked a strong possibility that he might have to resign. I'm sure Truman was aware of that."

and with the aid of police managed to make his way to the front tier area, where Bess was sitting. She tried desperately to reach him, but the surging and yelling crowd had the same idea. She was pushed back again and again. On the fifth try she succeeded. "Are we going to have to go through this all the rest of our lives?" Messall heard her ask her husband. Wisely, Truman didn't make any reply.

Ten guards were required to get the Trumans to their waiting car. Not much was said on the ride to the hotel. They were too tired. The next morning, Saturday, July 22, 1944, Bess held her first and last formal press conference. "I'm just getting excited," she told the reporters. She admitted that she had qualms about her husband being Vice-President. They asked her personal questions concerning Harry's food preferences, clothing styles, work routines. She replied that they were exactly like those of other Midwestern men. "He is the type of person," she said, "who would be delighted to eat beefsteak and fried potatoes every night."

The simple, unaffected man she described was in sharp contrast to the worldly-wise cosmopolite Truman would be running with. Harry added to Bess's homespun characterization when he burst into the room shouting for Margaret, "Where's my baby?" he yelled. "I have a message for her."

That afternoon the Trumans left for Independence. Soon after they arrived Bess and Harry visited neighbors on North Delaware Street. "They were the same plain couple they had always been," said one of them. "As a matter of fact Bess teased him for having worn a tie that clashed badly with his suit."

Those who didn't know the Trumans expected wholesale changes. "A few days later Bess went shopping in Kansas City," Ethel Noland said. "At the department store a woman recognized her and suddenly shrieked, 'It's Mrs. Truman!'

"'It can't be!' poohed another customer. 'She's only wearing seersucker!'"

Bess was too embarrassed to confirm or deny. She hurried out. When she got home, she told Harry about the incident. "I wonder if they thought a vice-presidential candidate's wife should be dressed in royal purple?" she said.

"That's when Harry got his dander up," Miss Noland recalled. "He raised his voice and shouted, 'If it had been a man I'd find him and . . . wring his fool neck!'"

Several weeks later Truman left for Washington to start preparing campaign strategy. At the time Roosevelt was in Hawaii, meeting with Admiral Nimitz and General MacArthur. When FDR returned to the White House, he dined with Harry on the terrace. While they snacked on sardines and toast, FDR said he'd be busy running the war and preparing the peace. He indicated that Truman would have to do most of the electioneering and asked how he thought it should be done. Harry replied that perhaps he might use an airplane.

Roosevelt promptly tabooed the idea. "One of us has to remain alive," he said.

When Harry got back to Independence, he spoke about Roosevelt's shocking appearance. Margaret said, "Father told how the President's hands shook so badly that he couldn't get the cream from the pitcher into his coffee. He spilled most of it into the saucer. He talked with difficulty."

Bess's advice was that Harry downplay the President's health. This time most of her counseling was long-distance. The Trumans had decided that she should remain in Washington to be with Margaret, who was a day student at George Washington University. "He phoned Bess nightly to give a progress report," said Hugh Fulton, who had resigned from the Senate Investigating Committee to serve Harry as chief advisor in Bess's absence.

"She may not have been there physically," Fulton said, "but she still made some very valuable suggestions. The Republicans were reluctant to attack Roosevelt's conduct of the war. They concentrated on his running mate and accused him of putting his wife on his Senate payroll. Bess had a simple, practical solution for that one. She told Harry to say that like most Americans, the Trumans weren't rich and that she had to work to make ends meet."

Bess also put a halt to some of her husband's silly-sounding shenanigans. When he phoned from Grand Forks, North Dakota, and described a war dance he had performed with Chief Standing Alone and four Sioux braves, she was appalled. "Harry," she admonished. "Remember what your mother said before you went on this trip?"

"What was that?" he asked.

"Behave yourself!"

Bess was equally chagrined when he told her about his behavior at a small Minnesota town that was enjoying a church fair. Truman was on his way to Minneapolis to address a rally that Hubert Humphrey had planned. Fulton had arranged for the train to stop briefly so that Harry could shake hands with people attending the festival. He couldn't resist entering a cow-milking contest, which he lost. ("Truman Loses—Battle of the Udders" ran a local headline.) He was also so carried away that he almost missed the Humphrey meeting.

Fulton said that once during the nightly call to Bess, Harry listened meekly to her exasperated scolding and finally said, "All right. All right. I promise I won't do it again." But he went on to engage in other hayseed stunts. The crowds seemed to like his corny approach. The Roosevelt-Truman ticket won handily—432 electoral votes to 99—very close to the figure Bess had cannily predicted. She was uncanny.

Truman had only been in office six days when Tom Pendergast died in Kansas City. It would have been wise politics to allow the death of the ex-convict politico to go unnoticed. Bess knew that wasn't her husband's style; above all else he believed in loyalty. Although she had never particularly liked Pendergast, she packed Harry's suitcase and took him to the airport, where he boarded an army bomber. After the brief Catholic service Truman told a reporter, "I'm sorry as I can be. He was always my friend and I have always been his."

Harry received a great deal of criticism because of his appearance. "He ought to have more sense," FDR told Sam Rayburn.

Sneered Senator John Bricker of Ohio, who had been Truman's Republican opponent for the vice-presidency, "Birds of a feather always flock together!"

Bess once pointed out that not everybody disagreed with Harry's final tribute to the dead boss. "The pro-letters he received," she said, "far outnumbered the one's condemning his actions. Thank goodness the American people still appreciate honest fidelity."

Through it all Truman remained unruffled. "If there is one thing I've learned about him," Snyder said, "it's his ability to shut things out of his mind if he feels he's in the right. He just went back learning to be Vice-President. He told Bess that his biggest beef was that he wasn't doing much. The two of them soon found out that Roosevelt was running a one-man show and that the job was mostly an honorary one, mostly socializing and hand-shaking."

That began immediately after the inauguration ceremony, when FDR retired to an upstairs White House room and left Eleanor, Bess and Harry to greet the guests. Sam Rayburn recalled that as he went through the lengthy receiving line, Bess, who had always been an avid baseball fan, said, "I feel like I'm pitching both ends of a double-header!" Later, as he was leaving, she wearily added, "Both games have gone extra innings!"

The Roosevelts rarely attended outside functions, and

Washington hostesses did the next best thing—they invited
Harry and Bess. The Trumans frequented so many affairs
that one columnist wrote: "The new Vice-President and his
lady have become the most sought-after couple in Washington. A day doesn't go by when they don't attend at least one
convivial soiree. Yesterday, they showed up at three."

Although the Trumans had become VIPs, Bess could
have appeared on an American Express commercial that
stressed nonrecognition. J. B. West, then the assistant to
the chief usher, said, "Mrs. Roosevelt held a luncheon for
top women in government. As I looked out the window
over the North driveway I spotted a short, grey haired
woman come up the steps. Mays, resplendent in his blue
tailcoat and white stockings, let her in. I stepped out of my
office and asked, 'Ma'am, your name?'

"'Mrs. Truman,' she said.

"Embarrassed, I led the wife of the Vice-President into
the Red Room."

Bess had always cherished anonymity. Suddenly everything changed. During her husband's ten years in the
Senate, she had only been known to her small circle of
friends. She rarely went to any of the lavish parties
Washington is noted for. She was a stickler for work.

Bess had grown accustomed to Harry bringing home a
bulging briefcase of unfinished work. After dinner the two
of them would clear the table and tackle the pile of papers.
Then they would discuss the next day's agenda, listen to the
radio and go to bed. Now Bess had to attend social
functions where she was required to serve as FDR's good-
will ambassador.

She once lamented to Ethel Noland, "I've begun thinking
that the ideal wife of a Vice-President should be skeleton-
thin. Only then would her constant party-going and command eating not become so apparent!"

"When Harry was elected to the new office, his salary
went up to $15,000," said John Snyder. "The raise, how-
ever, wasn't enough to drastically alter their standard of

living. The Trumans plus Mrs. Wallace, who was now living with them in Washington, continued to occupy a small apartment."

A friend of the Trumans described their living quarters. "It was the kind of place," she said, "where you put pretty slipcovers on to hide the Grand Rapids furniture."

Bess learned that her very modest wardrobe wasn't sufficient for her new social swirl when a society reporter wrote: "Yesterday the Vice-President's wife committed an unpardonable act. She appeared two days running in the same frock!"

Despite the "unpardonable act," the Trumans were adopted by Perle Mesta, the leading Washington hostess, who recognized their potential when they first arrived in the Capitol. She didn't monopolize them, but got to know them and waited. "Something in my bones told me that he was going places," she said later on. "I soon discovered it was a touch of rheumatism. But all kidding aside, for all he looks like a small town dentist, there was something about him that spelled success. Bess recognized it when they were only children."

Two-Party Perle, as the newspapers referred to her, was the daughter of an Oklahoma wildcatter who had struck it rich in oil. A marriage to a Pittsburgh steel magnate increased her fortune. And when she started making large political contributions, she really arrived. Her luxurious Washington home became a mecca for high government officials.

At her more casual parties, Harry played the piano and Fred Vinson sang "My Old Kentucky Home." While the exuberant duo was performing, Bess was in a corner exchanging ideas with Mrs. Mesta about religion. Perle, a Christian Scientist, later remarked, "She asked such intelligent questions—she could be a professor of theology. We had to stop when Harry and Fred tried to see who could sound the loudest."

"The reason they went to so many affairs," Vaughan

said, "was because Harry was so restless. But I guess he went to one too many. This time he went alone. The affair was the one given by the National Press Club. Harry agreed to play for the newspapermen and that's what brought on the fireworks!"

When Truman turned his back, actress Lauren Bacall jumped on top of the piano and swung her long legs as a photographer snapped away. The pictures made all the papers. An indignant Bess saw them. "She said she thought it was time for me to quit playing the piano at parties," a chastened Harry admitted.

For several weeks Truman was wary about any social piano-playing. His caution ended at a lavish ball given by Mrs. Gwendolyn Cafritz, Perle Mesta's archrival for the title of Washington social queen.

"Bess could tell how much he wanted to play," said Mrs. Cafritz. "I saw her nod her head to give him permission. He entertained us with selections from Chopin and Mozart. Bess looked especially lovely that night. Her blue eyes have always been her outstanding feature. But this time they really sparkled. So did everything about her."

That evening a member of the cast of *Oklahoma* who was also attending the Cafritz's party sang a medley of tunes from the hit Broadway show. Among them was "Everything Is Up to Date in Kansas City." When Bess was introduced to the performer, she said, "Not true. Nearby Independence is much more up to date. We have ice cream cones with three scoops."

Harry guffawed. "She sure is right," he said. "A town that produced her sure has to be up to date!"

At breakfast a few mornings later—April 12, 1945, eighty-two days after Truman became Vice-President—Bess reminded him that he owed his mother and sister a letter. That afternoon as he sat on the Senate rostrum, he composed a note:

Dear Mama and Mary,

I am trying to write you from the desk of the President of the Senate while a windy senator makes a speech on a subject with which he is no way familiar. . . . Turn on your radio tomorrow night at 9:30 your time, and you'll hear Harry make a Jefferson Day address to the nation. . . . I'll be followed by the President whom I'll introduce.

Truman never made that introduction. A few hours later Bess's husband was president of the United States.

IX THE RELUCTANT FIRST LADY

UNDEMONSTRATIVE BESS SOBBED and wept as she told Margaret that Roosevelt was dead. Harry had just called her from the President's office in the West Wing of the White House to say that FDR had died in Warm Springs, Georgia, at 4:35 P.M.

"I'm to be sworn in shortly," he said in an unusually low voice. "A car is on its way. Come as soon as you can."

Later Bess confided to Ethel Noland, "He sounded so shaken up and forlorn. My heart went out to him."

Quickly she and Margaret changed their clothes. Secret Servicemen led them to a rear entrance, because a large crowd had already gathered on the front lawn. Despite their attempted discreet departure, photographers surrounded the waiting limousine. Bess tried to ignore them as she pushed Margaret into a back seat. Silently they drove to the White House.

After paying their respects to Roosevelt's widow—Bess embraced Eleanor—they came down to the Cabinet Room to watch Harry sworn in as the thirty-third President. Frances Perkins, FDR's secretary of labor, witnessed the ceremony. She recalled it vividly as she looked at a photograph which had been taken during the historic event. Miss Perkins gave her observations to an interviewer from the Columbia University Oral History Project:

> I remember exactly how she looked that day. She had been crying. She had been weeping, and her eyes were red and swollen, and it was with difficulty that she kept her face straight from contortions of grief during the swearing-in. She's a quickly emotional person, and had naturally cried in her stress and her confusion, but she stood there like a Trojan, just startled and having to bear it, that's all. Her face shows it. It's a very interesting portrait, on that account.

At 7:08 P.M. Bess heard Chief Justice of the United States Harlan Stone administer the oath of office. He said, "I, Harry Shippe Truman . . ."

The outgoing Vice-President raised his right hand and repeated—with a slight change: "I, Harry S. Truman, do solemnly swear that I will faithfully execute the office of the President of the United States, and will to the best of my ability, preserve, protect, and defend the constitution of the United States. So help me God."

Bess allowed herself very brief mirth when Harry omitted the *Shippe*. Truman's parents had given him merely the initial *S* and left it to the family to guess which grandfather was meant, Solomon or Shippe?

Shortly after the ceremony Bess and Margaret left for the apartment. Harry remained behind to conduct a short cabinet meeting. When it was over Secretary of War Henry Stimson approached the new President, waiting until the others had left. He whispered that the United States was building a bomb that would be the most destructive weapon the world had ever seen and that would instantly end the war.

"I didn't know what he was talking about," Truman recalled. "But from the way he said it, I knew he wasn't ragging. Still, at the time, I had other things on my mind."

Secret Service guards surrounded the thirty-third President of the United States as he drove his own car home. It was 9:30 P.M. He found his wife and daughter in the next door neighbor's apartment. When Bess learned that he hadn't eaten since noon, she asked the neighbor, Mrs. Jefferson Davis, to fix him a turkey-and-ham sandwich and a glass of milk.

Truman gobbled the sandwich, drank most of the milk and announced that he was going to bed. Bess accompanied him back to their apartment. He was soon asleep. She said she spent most of the night thinking about how their lives would be changed. "I was very apprehensive," she admitted. "The country was used to Eleanor Roosevelt. I couldn't possibly be anything like her. I wasn't going down in any coal mines."

The following morning, Friday the thirteenth, Bess began her first full day as First Lady by cooking her husband's and Hugh Fulton's, who had joined him, breakfasts. After second cups of coffee they left for the White House. Bess made the beds, dusted the furniture and told Margaret to skip school for a few days. Then she telephoned friends in Independence and Washington. One of the calls was to Mrs. Davis, whom she thanked for her courtesy the previous night. She learned that the apartment house they lived in had practically become a fortress, protected by Secret Servicemen who allowed no one to enter without proper identification.

Many of the callers were practical-minded candidates for their soon-to-be-vacated $125 a month, rent-controlled apartment. The superintendent of the building said that during the first twenty-four hours there were more than a hundred applicants—about a dozen of the prospective tenants appeared between midnight and 6 A.M.

Bess didn't dare to venture outside because of the huge crowds of curious onlookers. She read a detective novel: *The Crimson Claw;* listened to the radio; made a shopping list. Late in the afternoon Harry phoned. She reminded him to tell Mrs. Roosevelt that they had no intention of moving into the Presidential quarters in the White House until the former First Lady had had time to decide what she intended to do. Bess said, "Be sure to tell her that she can remain there as long as she feels it is necessary."

Truman returned home shortly after 8 P.M. "He looked beat," Margaret recalled. "Mother helped him off with his jacket. You could tell he'd had a rough day—and that it wasn't over. He carried a briefcase filled with top-secret documents that he planned to read before morning."

The next day Roosevelt's body arrived from Warm Springs. Bess and Margaret joined Harry to attend the state funeral in the East Room of the White House. It was a very simple service and lasted only twenty-three minutes. Bess was composed now, but when Episcopal Bishop Angus Dun repeated the words from Roosevelt's first inauguration: "The only thing we have to fear is fear itself," her eyes grew moist again.

That evening the Trumans plus Roosevelt relatives, friends, government officials and diplomats boarded the funeral train that was to take the body to its final resting place on the banks of the Hudson River in Hyde Park, New York. Henry Wallace, one of the mourners, said, "It was a very hot night and sleep was hopeless. Although there weren't many stars out and no visible moon, I could see the silent, bowed crowds that lined the sorrowful tracks to pay tribute to their fallen leader as he made his last trip home. The train just crept along. Everything seemed dirgelike. Even the wheels sounded like so many muffled drums."

The next morning the train arrived at Hyde Park. An honor guard removed the coffin, which was placed on a horse-drawn caisson. The Trumans followed closely behind. When they reached the rose garden of the Roosevelt estate, eight servicemen lifted the bronze coffin to their shoulders and carried it to the grave site.

Bess looked startled when the first volley of the twenty-one-gun salute echoed across the Hudson valley. She reached for Harry's hand. The West Point band softly played Chopin's "Funeral March" and "Nearer My God to Thee." The mournful sound of taps marked the end of the ceremony.

On the return trip to Washington, Frances Perkins assisted Bess in making a decision that may well have set the style for Bess's reign as First Lady. In an interview for the Columbia University Oral History Project, the secretary of labor said:

> President Truman sent word he would like to see me. I came in [to the Truman compartment] and he was there with Mrs. Truman. We had a friendly talk about nothing special. While I was there somebody came in and said Mrs. Roosevelt was ready to see him. So he excused himself. . . .
>
> I sat there with Mrs. Truman awhile. She's very emotional, really. She felt terribly. She'd been all wrought up over the funeral and felt awfully about Roosevelt's death. She said to me, "I don't know what I'm going to do . . . I'm not used to this awful public life. Mrs. Roosevelt is on the way to Washington now and is going to pack up. She suggested to me that on Tuesday next I hold a press conference . . . She will sit with me and sort of introduce the girls to me and get me familiar with the procedure . . . Do you think I ought to see the press?" All this being said in a plaintive, emotional way.
>
> I had to think quickly, and I said, "No, Mrs. Truman, I don't think you ought to feel the

slightest obligation to do it. Mrs. Roosevelt is an unusual person. She had a special talent for publicity. She does it well. She enjoys it . . . I don't think any of the other First Ladies did it."

"Do you really think so?" she said. "You relieve me greatly, because I just thought I was going to be forced into this."

Mr. Truman came back into the compartment then, and she said to him, "Now, about this press conference—"

He said again, "Mrs. Roosevelt just tells me that she'll sit with you or introduce you to a press conference on Tuesday if you wish."

She said, "Well, I just asked Miss Perkins about it, and Miss Perkins thinks it's not necessary."

He said, "Well, I don't know." He asked me to say what I had told her again. I did, and then he said, "Well, I think she's right. There's no reason why you should do it, Bess."

When they returned to Washington, she drafted a note to Ruth Montgomery, who was then chairperson of Mrs. Roosevelt's Press Conference Association:

My dear Miss Montgomery:
I wish you would tell the members of your Association that I do not expect to hold press conferences.

I am hoping to see you a little later on after we move to the White House.

My husband and I deeply appreciate your good wishes and expression of admiration for us.

Very truly yours,
Bess W. Truman

Later the new First Lady arranged for her secretary to discuss the White House social calendar and occasionally replied to questions—submitted in writing. "But no direct interviews under any circumstances," she said flatly.

A reporter asked her, "Mrs. Truman, how are we ever going to get to know you?"

She quickly replied, "You don't need to know me. I'm only the President's wife and the mother of his daughter!"

On the Monday following Roosevelt's death, Bess, whom the press started calling stone-face, looked anything but— she looked euphoric—supremely happy as she waited for her husband to address a special session of both houses of Congress. She didn't appear to be very surprised when Harry duplicated his wedding performance of attempting to speak too soon. The microphones were turned on and everyone heard House Speaker Sam Rayburn whisper, "Just a minute. Let me present you, will ya, Harry?"

The speech was well received and was interrupted by frequent applause. When Truman finished, he was given a rousing ovation. Bess laughed as she told Rayburn that she hoped the honeymoon with Congress would last longer than the one Harry could afford when they were married.

She and Margaret then returned to the apartment, to supervise the move to new quarters. The Trumans felt that relocation was essential because their neighbors were constantly being harassed since they lived in the same building as the President of the United States. With Eleanor Roosevelt still occupying the White House, it had been decided that Blair House, diagonally across Pennsylvania Avenue from the Executive Mansion, could serve temporarily. It had been the residence of Francis Blair, of Andrew Johnson's Kitchen Cabinet, and his son, Montgomery Blair, who was postmaster general in Lincoln's administration. In 1942 the government had purchased it to lodge distinguished visitors.

Bess swiftly fell in love with Blair House. "Unlike the White House," she said, "it looks more like a home. In some ways it reminds me of our home in Independence—

not that our place is so elegant. But Blair House is gracious and warm and filled with graceful antiques."

The housekeeper, Mrs. Victoria Geney, found the new occupants "engaging." She said, "I was an employee but you would almost think it was the other way around. Mrs. Truman asked me, 'Are you sure it will be all right if we move in? I suppose we could stay on in the apartment since our rent is paid up until the end of the month. We don't want to cause you any inconvenience.' Imagine the wife of the President worrying if I would be troubled!"

A White House aide said Mrs. Truman was always like that. She had a deep concern for other people. Shortly after her husband became President, she heard that one of his assistants had fired several stenographers because they were helping Eleanor Roosevelt answer the stacks of condolence letters that poured in. Bess was appalled by this callous action and asked Harry to rehire the secretaries promptly and allow them to continue their work.

A few days after Truman was elevated to the Presidency, he decided that he needed a new press secretary. Charlie Ross, a Washington editor for the St. Louis *Post-Dispatch* and himself a man from Independence, was picked to fill the role. Ross recalled how it came about. "It was mostly Bess's notion," he said. "When Harry was fishing around for names, she tossed mine out. It meant a cut in salary, but they talked me into it. The three of us had been in school together. Little did I think the girl with the long blonde hair who sat in an up-front desk would one day get me into the White House's inner sanctum."

When Ross came to Blair House to say that he would take the position, he suggested to Bess and Harry that they break the news to Miss Tillie Brown, their high school teacher. "We placed a long-distance call," Ross said. "It was a touching moment when she replied, 'Just think, three of my favorite students at the head of the country. I'm proud of you all.'"

X "BESS WAS BEST"

Tuesday, May 8, 1945, always stood out in Bess's mind. Three very memorable events occurred during those twenty-four hours:

- V-E Day—the fighting in Europe officially ended.
- The President and his family spent their first complete day in the White House.
- It was Truman's sixty-first birthday.

"Harry may not have had a very large cake," Bess said later. "But he claimed that he had received half of the greatest birthday present anybody ever got—half the war was over. We sure were a beaming trio that day."

Washington gossip had it that the new First Lady wasn't happy very often, because she loathed living in the White House. "That simply was not so," said John Snyder. "She has always been a very private person. What seemed to be dislike of the quarters or bored disinterest was actually her way of avoiding being considered a celebrity. She looked up to other people, those she truly felt were important figures."

One of those she placed above herself was comedian Bob

Hope. Several days after the Trumans had settled into their new lodgings, the prominent comedian was invited to the White House to give a War Bond show. When Bess was introduced to him, she energetically pumped his hand and said, "Imagine having such a distinguished person call at your home. I guess the Presidency does have some exceptional compensations."

Margaret, too, was thrilled and started to say, "If I'd known you were coming . . ."

"You'd have baked a cake," he interrupted.

"No," Margaret replied. "I'd have brought my whole sorority."

Hope was delighted with her comeback. He laughed even louder when Bess said, "If your appearance had been publicized, I'm certain that the entire student body would try desperately to be pledged to Pi Beta Phi!"

"And she's not kidding!" added Harry.

Unlike Bob Hope's appearance, which ran smoothly, the next one, a presentation of actress Laurette Taylor in *The Glass Menagerie,* had a very stormy beginning—and almost didn't come off. Eddie Dowling, the producer of the hit Broadway show, recalled what happened in an interview at the Lambs Club in New York City for the Columbia University Oral History Project:

> We had received a command performance from Roosevelt. But he died. We decided to do it for the new President. On the way down, Laurette was drinking heavily. "I'm not going to meet this little pipsqueak from Missouri. I'm not going to the White House. My man is dead, and I'm not going . . ." And she carried on all the way down on the train. When we got to Washington, she and her boyfriend, Anthony Ross, who played the gentleman caller, went instead to a hotel. When I arrived at the White House without her, Mrs. Truman said, "Where is the great Miss Taylor?"

I explained that she had felt very close to Roosevelt.

"Well, that's a shame," she said. "Margaret and I have looked forward to this night, and we were going to have that nice little personal visit with her, and I'm terribly disappointed." So she poured the tea. Now we got our tea and little sandwiches and we were sitting down when the doors flew open and in came the mad Taylor.

With a great fanfare she said, "Well, here I am." Tony was dragging behind her with his coat dragging along the floor and the both of them half-plastered. "Tony told me this was a command performance. I take no commands from anybody. But he said that after all you are the President of the United States and I should be ashamed and here I am. I hope you'll understand. I was mad about Roosevelt. Roosevelt was the greatest man that ever walked the earth as far as I was concerned, even greater than Christ. So here I am in all my glory and ready to give a performance tonight the like of which you'll never see in your life—and I don't want any tea!"

So everybody laughed, and Mrs. Truman made her quite welcome. Oh, what a thoroughbred that Mrs. Truman was. And little Harry—he was the most gallant guy under these conditions. He said, "Well, I don't blame you, Miss Taylor. After all, you've come down here to a little understudy. That's all I am. And you know what an understudy is."

She said, "You're damn right I know what an understudy is. That so-and-so over there [pointing to me] has one sitting in the front row every time I go out onto the stage. Yes, that's what you are, an understudy. But I hope you're better than she is."

And more words to that effect. Well, it turned out to be a very fine performance. And Miss Taylor, bless her heart wherever she is at the moment, came around in great shape. After it was over she said, "You know, you're a great sport. You're okay. Why, if anybody did to me what I did to you, I'd throw him out. You're going to be a good President. Not as good as FDR. But then who could? But you're going to be a damn sight better than that understudy that son of a b got every night looking at me."

As Miss Taylor left, she turned to Harry and said, "By the way, that's a damn nice lady you're shacked up with!"

Shortly after her unorthodox histrionics, the prince regent of Iraq was invited to the Executive Mansion. His arrival was greeted with much pomp. As a strutting honor guard saluted His Royal Highness, a U.S. Navy band played the Iraqi National Anthem and the "Star Spangled Banner." Several dozen reporters covered the event. One of them said, "Mrs. Truman did the country proud extending a regal welcome tinged with Midwestern forthrightness."

That evening Harry invited the prince to a stag dinner. Bess was relieved that she didn't have to attend. However, she did comment about the absence of females. "The American system which calls for equality of women is undoubtedly superior," she said.

"In many ways Bess Truman was an early advocate of female rights," said India Edwards, director of the Women's Division of the Democratic Party. "She was instrumental in her husband appointing more women to top jobs than any previous President. There were nineteen women in key national posts and more than two hundred others as delegates, alternates or advisers to international conferences. Bess Truman earnestly believed that a woman is as good as a man—and she's the living proof."

Lillian Rogers Parks, a retired White House maid, endorsed Mrs. Edwards's point of view. "She always treated male and female employees in exactly the same way," she recalled. "And that was with enormous amounts of considerateness. She didn't keep looking over your shoulder the way Mrs. Eisenhower did, practically running over the furniture with white gloves looking for dust. Or Mrs. Roosevelt, who never looked to see if there was dust and we knew she didn't care. Of all the First Ladies I served in the White House, Bess was best!"

"It was the first house they ever had," said J. B. West, former chief usher. "Mrs. Truman's mother owned the one in Independence. True, the White House didn't actually belong to them, but as I told the First Lady, the President could use the place any way he wished, and every four years Congress allowed $50,000 above the annual appropriation to paint the house white and refurbish the interior. She could do quite a bit since Mrs. Roosevelt hadn't gotten around to doing it yet."

Mrs. Parks said that the Executive Mansion looked terrible when the Trumans moved in. "Right off she made some changes in the living quarters," she recalled. "It hadn't mattered much to the Roosevelts how the place looked, but it sure did to Mrs. Truman. She thought about it long and hard. Her bedroom was done in a rich shade of lavender. Her sitting room was painted a warm gray. She had the President's bedroom and his study painted in off-white. Very pleasant. Margaret's bedroom was done in a lovely shade of raspberry pink and her sitting room in light green. Mrs. Truman added flowers, pictures, new draperies and chintz slipcovers. She soon had the place looking more like a real home than it ever had before."

Just before the decorating had begun, Bess showed Harry some color chips. He pretended to look at them and then routinely said, "Yep, it's real nice. Use it." He repeated this several times.

Finally, Bess was exasperated. "Here's one that I'd like to do your study in," she said.

Once again the President replied automatically, "Yep, it's real nice. Use it." She started giggling. The paint chip was a vivid shade of shocking pink.

On June 2, 1945, Bess, Margaret and Mrs. Wallace left for Independence. When they arrived home, they were given an enthusiastic welcome. One boisterous greeter kept shouting, "Bess, it couldn't have happened to a more splendid lady!" The genial crowd seemed to agree. A bashful-looking youngster was suddenly thrust forward by her zealous mother to present the First Lady with a bouquet of roses. Bess plucked one of the flowers and handed it back to the awed child. The crowd applauded vigorously.

Before unpacking, Bess started phoning her neighbors. The next day she attended a session of the Independence bridge club and got her hair set at the local beauty parlor that she had frequented for years. "It was as if she never had been away," said her sister-in-law, Mrs. George Wallace.

Harry remained behind to attend the United Nations Charter Conference in San Francisco. "When Dad saw us off, he looked so forlorn we wanted to turn back," Margaret recalled. "We knew he'd be eating dinner in solitary state and wishing for us."

After addressing the last meeting of the UN conference, the President joined his family in Independence for a visit that the local newspaper called "the most monumental day Independence has ever had."

"Fortunately, the gala performance wasn't repeated each time the Trumans returned home," said Mrs. Haukenberry. "They let it be known that they hoped for some privacy, and most of the townspeople respected their wishes."

It wasn't the same in Washington.

"At the beginning Mrs. Truman tried to live as she had before her husband became President," West said. "It soon proved to be too difficult. She drove herself all around the district—to bridge games, Margaret's friends, homes of

Senate wives, to the beauty shop. She was like Mrs. Roosevelt in that respect—not caring for official limousines. But where Mrs. Roosevelt walked or took the bus, Mrs. Truman preferred driving—by herself.

"I remember her first call: 'Please have my car brought up at two o'clock,' she said.

"'Which one do you want?' I asked.

"'My own car, the Chrysler.'

"'Do you want a driver?'

"'Indeed not! I don't want to forget how to drive!'

"But that soon ended. Not long after she stopped at my office and said, 'I guess I'm going to have to stop driving my own car. It causes too great an uproar. When I stop at a light, people start running over. The Secret Service has laid down the law about my driving.'"

Subsequently Tom Hardy, Truman's driver during his eighty-two days as Vice-President, did her chauffeuring. Bess having a driver prompted a Washington cabby to send a letter to the editor of the *Post.* He wrote,

> I miss seeing Bessie Truman drive her big car all around town. She sure was skillful behind the wheel. How she could back up and park. It was a welcome sight for sore eyes. Let's face it she was a thousand per cent better than 99 per cent of the maniacs that fill the streets with their fancy, expensive cars. Well, I suppose that's the price you have to pay when you're married to the President.

The new First Lady avoided another "price" that was inflicted on her family. Franklin D. Roosevelt, Jr., had warned the Trumans about the food served at the White House. "It's terrible," he said. "But don't take my word for it. You'll soon find out firsthand."

Roosevelt's youngest son was quite right. Mrs. Henrietta

Nesbitt, the Executive Mansion's housekeeper, was in charge of the kitchen. "Her idea of what food should taste like," Bess told Ethel Noland, "would make eating in the poorhouse seem like dining in the Ritz!"

Mrs. Nesbitt had been brought into the White House by the Roosevelts, and she insisted on continuing their policy of *It's only food—why fret over it?*

When Bess tried to give her detailed instructions on what the menu should consist of, the housekeeper would sullenly reply, "Mrs. Roosevelt never did things that way!"

Several times Bess told Mrs. Nesbitt that the Trumans disliked brussels sprouts and not to serve them. This didn't seem to make any impression, and the detested vegetable continued to appear regularly at lunch and dinner.

The final straw occurred when Bess asked Mrs. Nesbitt for a stick of butter to bring to her Washington bridge club. "Oh, no!" exclaimed the housekeeper. "We can't allow any butter to leave this house! We've almost used up this month's ration stamps already!"

That night Bess related the incident to Harry; a few weeks later Mrs. Nesbitt retired. Her replacement was the assistant housekeeper, Mrs. Mary Sharpe, who found Bess an easy person to work for. "Mrs. Truman is a dear," she said. "She knows exactly what she wants and she tells you in a direct and respectful manner."

Mrs. Sharpe carefully arranged the daily menus to meet the Trumans' special nutrition needs: no salt was used because Bess had high blood pressure. The President was on a high-protein, low-calorie diet.

Before dinner Bess and Harry would go into the family sitting room in the West Hall to hold their nightly conference. Bess would ask Alonzo Fields, the head butler, to bring them two old-fashioneds. At the outset the proportion of bourbon in the drinks was not to her liking. She told Fields that she would appreciate it if he didn't make them so sweet.

He tried. Again, Bess felt they were too sugary. The next morning she expressed her distaste to the chief usher. "They make the worst old-fashioneds here I've ever had. They're like fruit punch."

The word got back to Fields, who prided himself on being a superb bartender. He decided that there was only one path left: he poured straight bourbon over the ice and brought the cocktails in.

Bess tasted her drink. She said jubilantly, "Now that's exactly the way we like our old-fashioneds!"

XI HOUSEWIFE #1, USA

SHORTLY AFTER TRUMAN assumed the Presidency, he went to Potsdam to meet with Winston Churchill and Joseph Stalin. Bess wouldn't let him fly. "People will think I'm a sissy!" he protested. "And besides, flying saves time."

"A ship is safer and will give you more time to think," Bess said. "And it's more dignified."

Reluctantly, he agreed to go on the U.S.S. *Augusta*. At the close of the conference, Harry arranged to return home aboard the *Sacred Cow*, the specially-equipped Presidential DC-4. With Bess several thousand miles away, he thought he was secure in coming to that decision.

He hadn't counted on the overseas telephone. Somehow his wife had learned of his intention. She called and insisted that he stick to his original plan to come home via ship. He objected, but she was insistent. Grudgingly he complied. "Okay," he finally said. "This time I'll do what you want, but you just don't realize how safe flying is. When I get back, I see I'll have to do some convincing."

He tried some months later. He decided to make a quick visit to Missouri to see his mother. He boarded the *Sacred*

Cow at Bolling Air Field, across the Potomac from Washington's National Airport. That day thousands of spectators were on their roofs watching an Air Force demonstration of P-80 fighter jets. Moments after Truman's takeoff he walked into the cockpit and said to the pilot, Colonel Hank Myers, "Mrs. Truman and Margaret are over there, standing on the roof of the White House. Do you suppose we could dive on them? Give them a few thrills?"

Myers, a daredevil flyer in his youth and still well known for airborne pranks, was squeamish about the request. Under protest he agreed. "Somebody's bound to catch hell for this," he said. "And I'm not going to take the blame."

"I've broad shoulders," Truman replied. "I'll take full responsibility."

Myers headed the plane toward Washington. Then he swooped, circled and dived, waggling wings as he buzzed the White House. Bess and Margaret were dumbfounded when they recognized the *Sacred Cow* and realized that Harry was on it. At first they were silent with terror. Then they waved weakly.

"I sure caught it when I got back," Harry recalled. "They bawled me out good. But it sure was worth it to see those two girls' faces."

"He was always doing things like that," said Mrs. Parks. "I remember when we'd be sweeping the rooms he'd break into a conspiratorial grin and say, 'Quick, we better sweep the dirt under the rug. Here comes the boss!' Soon we'd all be laughing."

"At breakfast he'd often tell Mrs. Truman things that happened during his early morning strolls. One time he came back chuckling a blue streak. It seems that when he was going down K Street, he spotted some people waiting for a bus. He took a place at the end of the line. First the man in front of him looked around, turned back, and then did a double take. A woman in line did the same thing. Soon the whole line was doing it. They would turn around, stare and shake their heads. That was when the President tipped his hat, said 'Good morning' and continued on his walk. He was real pleased with himself, and when he told Bess about it, she looked delighted, too.

"Then there was the incident about the ghost. One day two of Margaret's friends came over to spend the night. The three girls decided to sleep in Lincoln's oversized, lumpy bed. That's when the President got the idea about Lincoln's ghost. He asked Mays, the very tall butler, to put on a tail coat and stovepipe hat and start moaning in the corner of the room. It didn't come off only because Mays got sick that day. When Mrs. Truman found out about it, she laughed and laughed. 'Isn't that just like Harry?' she said admiringly."

Truman believed that fake spirits weren't always necessary in the Executive Mansion. "There are plenty of real ones," he said. He often talked about how Mrs. Calvin Coolidge claimed to have seen Lincoln's ghost. And that he himself had been awakened by a sharp knock at the door of his bedroom. "I went to investigate," he said. "No one was there. But I distinctly heard footsteps. Probably old Andy Jackson or some other ghost walking around."

Bess was interested, but at the time more concerned with live visitors. The White House was infested with rats; Mrs. Roosevelt told her that once she had given a luncheon for the wives of cabinet members when a huge rat ran boldly across the room. "All the ladies were terrified," she said. "We've tried exterminators. Nothing seems to help."

The new First Lady was very distressed. However, her sense of humor was still with her. "I suppose that's one way of getting rid of guests who have stayed too long," she said. The White House was completely rid of rodents only after the building was renovated during Truman's second term.

Although the war in Europe was over, the United States was still fighting the Japanese. Bess was invited to christen two Navy R-5D hospital evacuation planes that had been bought from the proceeds of War Bond sales by the Congressional Wives Club.

"In sending forth these planes," she said with great dignity as she held a champagne bottle aloft, "we send them with our love and sincere desire that the wounded whom they carry will be brought safely home." Then she swung the bottle. Unfortunately it hadn't been properly scored, and despite vigorous slamming it refused to break. Bess's face reddened.

Margaret, who had been asked to be an attendant-in-honor, recalled that she thought the planes would never leave the ground. After six failures she whispered to her now exasperated mother, "Fine thing for a former shot-put champion."

"Be quiet," Bess hissed and tried again. Ultimately a navy lieutenant stepped forward and hit the bottle with a hammer. The bottle broke, but Bess's trim black dress was soaked with champagne.

Harry heard about her near-defeat, and that evening at dinner he teased his wife. "And I always thought you had a strong right arm from playing tennis," he said.

Bess looked indignant. She started to toss a bread crumb in the President's direction, but reconsidered. Instead she put it in her mouth. "You're lucky we mustn't waste food!" she said.

The Trumans' meals were far from elaborate. Bess felt that due to wartime austerity her family should eat the same food other Americans put on their table. "They look to us," Charles Ficklin, a White House butler, heard her say. "We have to set a good example, so stew and beans it is!"

She proposed to Harry that he urge housewives to conserve food so that starving victims throughout the world could be fed. The President agreed with his wife and asked her to lead the way. A food pledge was prepared, and she was one of the first to sign it. Her vow was featured in newspapers throughout the country:

> The Pledge of the American Housewife
> 1. I will do my utmost to conserve any and all foodstuffs which the starving millions of the world need today so desperately.
> 2. I will buy only the food my family actually needs for its proper nourishment and health.
> 3. I will neither waste nor hoard . . . nor discard any article of food . . . in cooking or in serving . . . and will ask my family for the fullest cooperation.
> 4. I will be particularly watchful in the use of Wheat and Cereals . . . and Fats and Oils . . . and will try to make certain that not a scrap of Bread is wasted in my home.
> 5. I will make these little sacrifices gladly . . . for the sake of those who cannot enjoy my God-given right to live . . . and give . . . as an American.
>
> *Bess W. Truman*
> 1600 Pennsylvania Avenue
> Washington
> (Mrs. Harry S. Truman)

(June 7, 1946)

"Mrs. Truman took that pledge very seriously," said Ficklin. "She was mighty pleased when the post office delivered a letter to her that was marked Housewife # 1, U.S.A. She gave strict orders that the White House staff follow her pledge exactly. The way she eyed the menus you'd think she was putting them through a strainer. She never allowed us to violate her promise by as much as a teaspoon of butter or a slice of bacon. I don't think any American woman gave her word of honor with a more willing heart. We had substitutes for beef all the time—

canned salmon, for example; and the ends of bread went into the meat loaf."

During the food-conservation crusade she and Mrs. John Snyder, an old friend and wife of Truman's secretary of the treasury, were dining in a small Washington, D.C., restaurant. They ordered salads, but the waitress had other ideas. "For the President's wife and her companion," she whispered, "we have two nice, juicy steaks."

"Bring us two salads, please!" Bess said firmly. "And do remember, there is a beef shortage even for the President's wife!"

Later that afternoon she and Mrs. Snyder went shopping for dresses. One of the stores they visited was a boutique that prided itself on catering to Washington's elite. "There's no use for me to try anything here," Bess said. "I can't possibly afford your prices." The salesgirl suggested that the First Lady open up a charge account. "Thank you just the same," said Bess. "I never charge!"

When she was in her twenties and early thirties, Bess had shown a great interest in modish dressing, studied fashion magazines and, according to her mother, was "a great fusser" about her appearance. After her marriage she dressed very conservatively. In public she was usually seen in a kind of uniform of dark blue suit, white blouse and dark blue accessories. Invariably she wore white gloves and comfortable shoes. With indifference, she dressed in the same costume on successive occasions. Her favorite clothes came from a family department store in Kansas City where the same salesgirl had waited on her for years.

"I don't remember ever selling Mrs. Truman anything flashy," she said. "She wanted good, strong, conservative respectability. She'd be caught dead before she'd appear in public in hems above the knees à la Mrs. Kennedy. Or the idea of a facelift job like the one Mrs. Ford got. Perish the thought!"

Bess was aware that style setters often referred to her as dowdy. She thought about changing but always returned to the dark blue suit.

"Why don't you buy a new suit?" she was asked.

"But I've got a suit!" she replied.

She once telephoned Mrs. Byron Price, whose husband, the director of censorship, was going to receive an award from the President. To Mrs. Price she said, "This is Bess Truman. I understand you are coming to the White House to the ceremony to honor your husband. I decided to phone you to ask you what you are going to wear. I want to dress as you do. I do hope it's nothing elaborate."

Bess felt that fancy designer dresses just wouldn't look right on her 140 pound, 5-foot-4 frame. And after all, Harry had said repeatedly, "She looks just like a woman ought to look who's been happily married for a quarter of a century."

XII FORSAKING ALL OTHERS

"WHEN TRUMAN BECAME President, it became important to me to learn about his sex life," said Walter Trohan, former Washington bureau chief of the Chicago *Tribune*. "In the first weeks I went to Representative Paul Shafer of Michigan to demand the complete story of what went on in Costa Rica and Mexico, during a joint junket of the Senate and House Armed Services committees. Truman was a member of the group, as well as the Republican Shafer."

The veteran journalist had heard numerous smirking remarks about that now-infamous congressional jaunt, but until Roosevelt's death the details hadn't interested him. "Now I felt I had to know for future guidance," he said. "Shafer agreed to discuss the trip with me."

He told Trohan that in San José, the capital of Costa Rica, they had been tended an opulent Presidential dinner with a large variety of alcoholic drinks. At the conclusion of the meal, the lawmakers were taken to an exclusive country club on the outskirts of the city, where they were introduced to a group of attractive young ladies they assumed to be the wives and daughters of their Latin American hosts. They learned differently when a prominent senator, who had been drinking a great deal of tequila, suddenly reached down the front of a low-cut gown. Instead of being offended, the woman burst out laughing and put her arms around the drunken lawmaker.

The legislators quickly learned that the female guests weren't related to South American bigwigs but were high-class prostitutes who had been hired to entertain the distinguished visitors from the north. Soon a full-scale orgy was in progress.

"When one of the ladies of the night approached Truman, he rose and rushed out to his waiting car," said Shafer. "The chauffeur drove him back." The Michigan representative added, "For the rest of the trip, Truman slipped away from similar amusements the lawmakers devised in other cities. His conduct throughout was always that of the exemplary husband and father."

"I'm sure Harry never told Bess anything about that part of the trip," said Snyder. "It was not his way. He always believed that a gentleman never discussed anything off-color in the presence of a woman. That principle was sacred to him. He treated it so earnestly that if there were even the slightest hint of a ribald joke upcoming, he would quickly put a stop to it if Bess or Margaret was in the room."

Once at a small White House reception, a high-ranking government official said, "Did you hear about the traveling salesman . . ."

He got no further. Harry put up his hand and stopped him in midstream. "None of that here!" he exclaimed. "Don't you know there are ladies present?"

The startled near-offender was flabbergasted. Later he told the President that all he was going to say was that various types of traveling salesmen were becoming obsolete. Harry's answer was that the mere mention of "traveling salesman" suggested a bawdy joke and should be avoided when ladies were around.

Yet Truman liked to create the impression that he was sexually sophisticated. At a lavish and diplomatically ticklish state dinner for General Charles de Gaulle, he turned to former Secretary of Labor Lewis Schwellenbach and sighed, "Instead of being President I should have been a piano player in a bordello!"

A much-jolted Schwellenbach replied, "Well—er—that would have been too bad, because then we would never have known you."

Truman's reply was even more surprising. "Why be so high and mighty?" he said. "As though you've never been in a whorehouse!"

House Speaker Sam Rayburn wasn't too surprised. He said, "Among men that was sometimes Harry's style—pretending he was worldly-wise. But that didn't fool anyone. Everybody in Washington knew that for him there was only one girl—Bess. The only person stupid enough to try and link Harry with a woman other than his wife was Richard Nixon. It took place when Helen Gahagan Douglas was running against Nixon for a Senate seat. He didn't come right out and say it—that's not his way. Instead, the oily jackass implied that the only reason Truman was backing her was due to a romantic relationship."

Rayburn told how Nixon accomplished this. At one large campaign rally in a Los Angeles suburb, he answered a planted question from the floor: "I'm not suggesting that any hanky-panky is going on between Harry Truman and my opponent. But lots of knowledgeable people claim where there is smoke there must be fire!"

The House Speaker was an unusually kind-spoken person, but he'd lose his composure when discussing Nixon. "The kindest explanation I have for that ugly-faced monster," said Rayburn, "is that he was born without a heart. He knew full well that Bess has always been Harry's one and only!"

Her thoughts about the human body and sexual matters

closely paralleled her husband's: "A person's anatomy was a very private affair and never, never was the concern of an outsider!"

It was demonstrated by an incident that occurred at Shangri-La, the Presidential retreat currently known as Camp David. The First Lady often used the Catoctin Mountain sanctuary, which is about sixty-five miles from Washington, for informal luncheons. Commander William Rigdon, one of Truman's military aides, recalled, "Once she was entertaining some of her friends and asked me to send everything over to the swimming pool. She explained that she didn't want any stewards detailed to serve. The ladies would take care of the service themselves. I got the idea all right. Or so I thought.

"It happened that I received an urgent call from the White House, which necessitated that I summon her. I made my approach as noisily as I could, but nevertheless arrived unnoticed to confront eight mature ladies sitting in a line on the pool's edge, fully clothed except for shoes and stockings, dangling their feet in the water and apparently having a grand time."

All the White House employees were aware of the deep love and respect Bess and Harry had for each other. "I never did see anybody more devoted to another person than they were," said Mrs. Parks. "One day the President was in the Oval Office when he got a call saying that Mrs. Truman had suddenly taken ill and felt faint. At the time they were living in Blair House. He tore out of the White House and ran across Pennsylvania Avenue with honking cars almost on top of him. How that man ran. The Secret Service were in hot pursuit, but they couldn't possibly catch him. It was a scene that only Hollywood could do justice to. Fortunately it was only a virus, and Mrs. Truman soon recovered."

Bess acted the same way when, in Harry's second administration, two Puerto Rican nationalists tried to storm

Blair House to assassinate the President. They succeeded in
killing a guard and seriously wounding two others. The First
Lady, who was dressing to attend a dedication commemora-
tion at Arlington Cemetery, heard the gunshots and rushed
to her husband's side to shield him from possible harm. At
the time he was in an adjoining bedroom.

After the tragic episode the Secret Service put more men
on constant guard. That evening Mrs. Truman went through
the building and grounds and counted them. "Not enough!"
she said. "We need more men on duty!"

Mrs. Parks said, "For months she watched over her
husband like a mother tiger."

Once when the Trumans went for a holiday with friends
Dorothy and Samuel Rosenman, photographers snapped a
picture of Mrs. Rosenman and Truman swimming together
in a pool. The caption gave the impression that they were
vacationing without their spouses. Bess laughed when she
saw the picture and said, "Dorothy's a very nice woman,
but I'm afraid Harry's spoken for."

Truman's mammoth adoration for his wife—and hers for
him—was continuously subject to speculation. Mrs. Parks
said, "At first those of us who served them wondered how
such totally different people got together. It was a deep
mystery, but we finally decided that it was the bad little boy
in Harry Truman that appealed so much and made her
choose him.

"You might call it a Victorian-type marriage—that is, if
those Victorians weren't such prudes. In private the Trumans sure weren't. I remember once they had been apart
for about two weeks because Bess had been visiting
Independence. Right after she returned a bed slat broke
and had to be replaced. Next day the President kept
strutting around, acting real proud. Mrs. Truman, who is
very shy in public, kept blushing like a new bride, but I had
the feeling that she was pleased. It's impossible to think of
one without the other!"

Both Trumans firmly expressed themselves on divorce: they were strongly opposed to it. They were very disturbed when it happened to anyone they knew. Harry told author Merle Miller, "Right after the war, he [Eisenhower] wrote a letter to General Marshall saying that he wanted to be relieved of duty, saying that he wanted to come back to the United States to divorce Mrs. Eisenhower so that he could marry this English woman . . . It was a very shocking thing to have done."

Bess may have well been referring to Ike when she told Ethel Noland, "Marital partners sometimes treat a sanctified union much too lightly. They don't even try to work things out before heading for the divorce court . . . They allow trouble to seep in when they've been apart for long periods."

"The Trumans rarely were apart," John Snyder said. "The reason they spent so much time together was very simple—they enjoyed each other's company. With Margaret they formed a self-sustaining unit. Whenever anyone was absent, there was a daily telephone call."

As a rule, Bess steered clear of other families' personal affairs. She made an exception when the daughter of a distant cousin contemplated divorce. Bess invited the young woman to tea. "She didn't ask me about my marriage right out," the woman said. "But she was so gracious and understanding that I soon found myself pouring out all the gory details. I don't think she was too eager to hear them. Nevertheless, I went on and on. She didn't say much—just listened and responded quietly with the right amount of gravity and piousness. I don't mean to say that when she talked, she talked a lot about God. She didn't have to—I could tell her faith was playing an important role.

"The more she listened, the more I confided. Just poured it out. After a while I discovered that a great deal of the trouble was caused by me. I'd be wrong if I said Mrs. Truman solved all my problems single-handed—a trained counselor and my own subsequent hard work were necessary for that. But I do believe that I wouldn't have consulted him if she hadn't taken the time to hear me out. She's a Christian in the true sense of the word."

Robert Hart, the rector of the church Bess was confirmed and married in, said, "I'd describe Bess Truman as a deeply religious person. She doesn't practice being a good Christian on Sunday and then forget about it the following days of the week. She takes her religion seriously."

Bess was once awarded a scroll for "brotherhood" by a group of Jewish women. During dinner she told the chairperson, "Perhaps my husband's Grandfather Young put it best when he said, 'Watch out for the man who spends the Sabbath praying and howling. When he's around, you better go home and lock up your smokehouse.' I suppose that's also been my philosophy—*a quiet faith.*"

XIII MEANWHILE, BACK AT THE WHITE HOUSE

SEVERAL MONTHS AFTER the Trumans settled into the Executive Mansion, Edith Helm, Bess's social secretary, said the First Lady started following a fairly regular schedule:

7:15 A.M.—Awakened by clock radio playing soft music. After washing she would don a simple housedress and join Harry and Margaret for breakfast.

8:00 A.M.—The morning meal usually included hot popovers, sorghum molasses and much lively talk.

9:00 A.M.—Took elevator to her tiny second floor office where daily appointment sheet and menus would be presented to her. Briefed Mrs. Helm and later Miss Odlum on what social information they should release to the press. Future White House plans discussed.

10:15 A.M.—Five-minute recess, then continued working at her desk. Helped secretary draft letters, but insisted on answering all personal mail in longhand. Carefully verified all bills and wrote every check. Made numerous phone calls. Visited her mother's room.

11:00 A.M.—(Mondays only.) Attended Spanish class.

1:00 P.M.—Lunch. Usually with President. If he had other plans she would eat alone or in her mother's room. Once a week dined with friends.

2:00 P.M.—Retired to her sitting room. Read a mystery story. Listened to Washington Senators baseball game on radio.

3:00 P.M.—Received delegations. Entertained servicemen. Made appearances at "required" receptions: charity, public health, nutrition, important wives . . .

6:00 P.M.—Cocktails and conversation with Harry—always just one substantial 2½ ounce drink apiece, usually bourbon old-fashioneds.

7:00 P.M.—Dinner served by formally dressed butlers to informally dressed Trumans. In good weather would eat in the South Portico. Typical meal:

Fruit Cup
Pork roast
Apple sauce   Creamed peas
Buttered carrots
Chocolate cream pie
Coffee, buttermilk

8:00 P.M.—Often viewed films. Margaret was a

movie buff and urged parents to watch them with her—she saw *The Scarlet Pimpernel* starring Leslie Howard sixteen times. Some evenings Bess would challenge Margaret and her daughter's friends to a Ping-Pong match or a game of bridge.

9:00 P.M.—Arm-in-arm, Bess and Harry would stroll to his study, shut the door and engage in the second half of their daily conference.

11:00 P.M.—Bedtime. Read until midnight.

"There were mighty few times when Mrs. Truman made changes in her schedule," said Charles Ficklin. "It was so regular that you could almost set your watch by it."

White House servants recalled that the night before the dropping of the second bomb—this time on the Japanese city of Nagasaki—Bess and Harry remained in his office for their nightly council much longer than the usual period. "When they came out at last," said Ficklin, "they both looked real serious. Usually they'd joke or kid around before going off to bed. Now they didn't say a word, just looked straight ahead, downright glum."

Marianne Means, a Washington-based reporter, interviewed Truman for her book *The Woman in the White House*. She asked him what role his wife played in his Presidency. "Truman told me," Miss Means said, "that Bess was a full partner in all his transactions—political and otherwise. He acknowledged that he consulted her about some of the great decisions of American history, such as should we use the atom bomb?"

Other than Harry's statement to Miss Means that he and Bess discussed whether to use the atom bomb, there is very little information about the First Lady's role, if any, in his determination to employ the weapon. Yet Truman said again and again: "I never make a decision unless Bess is in on it." It's hard to believe that he didn't consult her on something that important.

One of the few times Bess talked about the bomb was to a member of her bridge club, several years after the President had retired. She said, "Harry always placed high value on the life of a single American boy. If the war with Japan had been allowed to continue, it would have claimed the lives of perhaps a quarter-million American soldiers, and twice that number would have been maimed for life. It's difficult to calculate the number of Japanese lives that would have been lost . . . as many or more, undoubtedly, as died at Hiroshima and Nagasaki. So the atom bomb was the lesser weapon, although it's hard to look at it that way."

Five days after the Nagasaki holocaust the Japanese government surrendered unconditionally. A cheering crowd that was hear hysteria gathered outside the White House. Bess and Harry went out to greet them and kept making V-for-victory signs. The jubilant celebrators responded by shouting, "President Truman forever!"

Bess whispered, "Perish the thought."

The mob kept yelling, and the Trumans continued flashing the victory sign. Finally Bess and Harry were allowed to go back inside. They headed for the Oval Office, where they broke their one-drink-a-day rule.

"The following morning it was business as usual for Mrs. Truman," said Edith Helm. "I don't think she enjoyed being subject to a fixed routine. But even with her regular schedule, she managed to include some variety. She certainly took delight in her Spanish class. She read quite well but didn't get enough practice speaking to be fluent."

Bess was a star pupil. Her interest in the language began when Harry was a senator. She enrolled in a course conducted at Washington's Hotel Shoreham, and when her husband became President, she had the class transferred to the White House. Every Monday morning the class met in the Green Room. At the outset her fellow students included

Mrs. Dwight Eisenhower; Mrs. Robert Patterson, wife of
the secretary of war; Mrs. Tom Clark, wife of the attorney
general; Mrs. Lester Pearson, wife of the Canadian ambassador; Mrs. Dean Acheson, wife of the undersecretary of
state; Mrs. Lister Hill, wife of the Alabama senator;
Representative Jessie Summer of Illinois; and Raethal
Odlum, a social secretary.

The instructor was Ramón Ramos, a Cuban and president of the Pan American Club of the YMCA. He said,
"Mrs. Truman is a very bright student. And what's even
better, she always comes to class with her homework fully
prepared."

During Pan American week the group decided to cook a
typical south-of-the-border meal. They took over the White
House kitchen, and with Professor Ramos shouting instructions—in Spanish—they merrily prepared a luncheon with a
Latin-American flavor.

The main dish was *picadillo*. The class chopped and
mixed four varieties of meat with rice. They seasoned the
mixture with hot spices and plenty of garlic. They garnished
it with almonds, pimento, olives and raisins. The dessert
was a mixture of Mexican cheeses and guavas in syrup.
Some of the students put on aprons and did the serving; the
rest sang a medley of Spanish songs.

Because of Bess's deep interest in Latin America, Ambassador Guillermo Belt of Cuba announced that he would
present to the First Lady the Carlos Manuel de Cespedes
award—the highest honor given to a foreigner. Harry felt
that when Bess accepted the medal, it would be nice if she
made a short thank-you speech in Spanish.

"I never make one in English," she said, "let alone in
another language!"

When she realized that her husband was disappointed,
she agreed to write one out in English and have Professor
Ramos translate it into Spanish. At each class session
preceding the ceremony, Bess rehearsed the short address

in front of the group, with one of the students acting the part of the ambassador. Although she was well prepared she was extremely nervous when the day finally arrived. Ambassador Belt commented that she did just fine.

"I'm so glad you understood it," Bess said. "My daughter says my accent is atrocious."

The President, who attended the ceremony, didn't agree at all. "Isn't she terrific?" he said admiringly. "I didn't understand a word!"

Shortly after Harry's enthusiastic tribute to his wife, she received one from a Methodist minister who praised her for ordering orange juice instead of a cocktail as the first course of a charity luncheon. "Mrs. Truman is a true-blue credit to American womanhood," the clergyman said fervently.

When Bess returned to the White House, she told Alonzo Fields, the head butler, "I guess I'll now have to stick to orange juice so that I'll continue to be true-blue." She noticed how pained he looked and with a straight face and deadpan expression added, "On second thought that would not allow you to make use of your bartending skills. You'd be sad, and we can't have that. I suppose the President and I will have to order two of your delicious old-fashioneds!"

Harry took the drink when it was served, thanked Fields and informed Bess that to him she'd always be true-blue, but that he would have to be away for part of the visit her Independence bridge club was making to the White House the following month. "I don't like leaving," he told her. "But I'm afraid it's necessary."

Then, as many husbands have done under similar circumstances, he got out of the house when the women arrived. He went to Hyde Park to dedicate FDR's birthplace as a national shrine. Meanwhile Bess entertained ten of her hometown friends. For twenty-five years the Tuesday bridge club of Independence had been gathering bimonthly for lunch and then stakeless bridge. But never in its long and gossipy career had it ever enjoyed a meeting like the one Bess had arranged.

During a four-day stay the ladies ate in the state dining room, had high tea at Blair House, sat in the Presidential box at Constitution Hall for a concert, visited the President's Oval Office, saw a circus—and some of them even slept in Lincoln's bed. They also found time for two quick rubbers of bridge.

"The only near-mishap occurred when we went to see the Shriner Circus," recalled Mrs. Thomas Twyman, who was a member of the group. "Bess was feeling especially cheerful until a clown tried to sit on her lap. 'That will be enough!' she said firmly. It was one of the very few times I ever saw her even slightly cross. When she was really displeased, Harry let everyone know."

Twice that resentment was made public and both times resulted in the culprits who had caused the annoyance being permanently barred from the White House. One incident occurred when the First Lady planned to be a guest at a tea given in Constitution Hall by the Daughters of the American Revolution. The item appeared in the newspapers just after the DAR refused to allow black pianist Hazel Scott to use Constitution Hall for a concert. A great ruckus arose over Bess's apparent endorsement of the DAR's antiblack position, and Miss Scott's husband, Democratic Representative Adam Clayton Powell of New York, referred to Bess as the Last Lady of the Land. He pointed out that her predecessor, Eleanor Roosevelt, had resigned from the DAR in 1939 when it refused to allow black singer Marian Anderson to use their Constitution Hall.

Earlier Bess had sent Powell a telegram explaining that her date to attend the tea was made before the "unfortunate controversy arose" and was not related to the merits of the issue. "Personally," she added, "I regret that a conflict has arisen for which I am in no wise responsible. In my opinion my acceptance of the hospitality is not related to the merits of the issue which has since arisen . . . I deplore any action which denies artistic talent an opportunity to express itself because of prejudice against race or origin."

Harry was less charitable and refused to offer Powell any explanation. The congressman had been rude to Bess— henceforth Powell would be excluded from all White House lists.

Another person who was never allowed to set foot in the Executive Mansion was Clare Boothe Luce, publisher of *Time* magazine. Mrs. Luce had made scornful remarks about Bess. "No one could do that and get away with it," said General Vaughan. "Harry regarded that as the equivalent of spitting on the flag. Once Henry Luce asked why President Truman bore the grudge. 'Mr. Luce,' Harry replied, 'you've asked a fair question and I'll give you a fair answer. I've been in politics a long time and everything that could be said about a human being has been said about me. But it's different with my wife. She has always conducted herself in a circumspect manner and no one has a right to make derogatory remarks about her. Now your wife has said many unkind and untrue things about Mrs. Truman. And as long as I am in residence here, she'll not be a guest in the White House.'"

Whenever possible, Bess helped calm down her often obstreperous husband. An opportunity occurred when the Soviet Embassy advised the United States that Ambassador Nikolai Novilkov couldn't attend Truman's first diplomatic dinner. "Due to illness," was the excuse they gave.

The "illness," the State Department quickly learned, was purely political. The Lithuanian envoy-in-exile had also been invited, and he was *persona non grata* to the Russians, as they had just occupied his country. Truman felt the refusal showed disrespect to Bess, who had been working painstakingly on the affair. He wanted Novilkov expelled from the United States immediately. Dean Acheson, who was then undersecretary of state, rushed over to the White House and tried to reason with the President, pointing out that the proposed action would surely have international reverberations. But Truman remained adamant. "It's not only an insult to the country," he shouted. "It's an insult to my wife!"

That's when Bess, who had heard the commotion, decided to intervene. She telephoned him from her tiny upstairs office. Acheson recalled that the President listened meekly as she apparently read the riot act to him.

"All right. All right," he said resignedly. "I know when I'm licked. Let's forget all about it." He hung up the receiver and picked up a photograph framed in gold filigree from the top of his desk. He handed it to Acheson. It was a picture of a young woman. The President said, "Look on the back." There was written: *Dear Harry, may this photograph bring you safely home from France—Bess.* It was dated 1917. "Any so-and-so who is rude to that girl is in big trouble with me!" Truman ended.

As Acheson was leaving, the President called, "Tell old Novocaine we won't miss him!"

XIV "OKAY, YOU MAY RUN"

"ASIDE FROM CLARE Boothe Luce and Adam Clayton Powell, everyone else was made welcome in the White House," said Charlie Ross. "Even Republicans were invited to call. Former President Herbert Hoover had been snubbed by Roosevelt—not so with Truman when he took over the office. Just after Harry moved in he encouraged Hoover to visit and give him deferential treatment. I believe the idea came from Bess and her mother, who greatly admired the former President."

The conversation got around to fishing. Hoover, who had always been regarded as an exceptional angler, said that a proper grandfather had to take his grandchild fishing. "Well, in that case," Truman remarked. "I guess Bess will have to be the proper grandfather. When we were younger, she was the one who took me fishing."

In the next few months many other VIPs visited the White House. They represented a very broad spectrum— from the Soviet Foreign Secretary Vyacheslav Molotov to then child star Elizabeth Taylor. Not all of them may have agreed with United States policy, but they were unanimous in their praise of the First Lady. Molotov, who could be quite brusque, didn't sneer outright at capitalism when he visited the Executive Mansion. However, he did say that the bread in his country was superior. But then he added that Mrs. Truman was "a good woman."

Thirteen-year-old Elizabeth Taylor participated in a White House broadcast for the infantile paralysis fund-raising campaign and traded autographs with the First Lady. Bess offered to "throw in the President's autograph" because she felt she was getting the better of the deal. The youngster quickly replied, "No, Mrs. Truman, that won't at all be necessary. You're so well-liked in Hollywood that I'm sure I can even get a Clark Gable in trade for this one of yours!"

Bess escorted Premier Alcedi De Gasperi of Italy and his daughter, Maria, on a tour of the White House. The Italian leader kissed Mrs. Truman's hand and said, "The most charming feature of this charming house is undoubtedly yourself!"

His Royal Highness the Crown Prince of Saudi Arabia was even more elegant in his praise of the First Lady. Upon leaving the White House he bowed low and said, "Your very blue eyes sparkle so brightly that they match the very sky when it shines the brightest."

Winston Churchill, who stopped off on his way to make the ominous "Iron Curtain" speech in Fulton, Missouri, complimented Harry "on having availed yourself of a splendid helpmeet that is fit for a king."

Harry loved to hear dignitaries laud his wife. However, he was also pleased when the flattery included a bit of humor. Roosevelt's grandson, Johnny Boettiger, had been hospitalized when FDR died at Warm Springs and his grandmother and mother moved out of the White House. They had inadvertently left behind some of his most cherished possessions. He asked President Truman if he could look for them. Harry insisted on helping. Together they searched all the wardrobes. In one that belonged to Bess, Johnny parted the hanging dresses and looked on the floor in the back. When he emerged, he said, "I'm sure your wife is a very nifty person, but her closets are just as messy as Grandma's."

Truman repeated the story to Bess. She laughed and said, "Well, I'm pleased that I resemble Mrs. Roosevelt in at least one respect."

"He broke up when she said that," Ross recalled. "The only other time I heard him laugh so hard was at a garden party that Jim Byrnes attended."

When Secretary of State James Byrnes returned to Washington from a trip he made to Moscow as Truman's personal emissary, he was roundly panned by the press. On his homecoming, the Trumans gave a lawn party for wounded servicemen and invited Byrnes to stand with them in the receiving line. Most people brushed right past the secretary. One private first class, however, shook his hand furiously. "Gosh, sir," he said. "You did a wonderful job for us in Russia!"

Byrnes was delighted finally to hear a kind word about his much-criticized mission. "Why, thank you, soldier. Where are you from?"

"St. Elizabeth," the young man said.

Bess was told about the conversation by Ruth Montgomery, a Washington journalist, who had overheard the exchange. "Mrs. Truman was very amused," said Miss Montgomery. "St. Elizabeth was a government hospital for the mentally disturbed. 'I can't wait to tell Harry,' the First Lady said. 'This will simply make his day.' She made a beeline directly to the President, and soon the two of them were laughing heartily."

Reporters who learned about the incident felt that Bess was finally mellowing. They started pressuring Mrs. Helm, her social secretary, into arranging a face-to-face press conference. The First Lady flatly refused. After more

Right: Martha Ellen Young and John Anderson Truman, Harry's parents. *Courtesy Harry S. Truman Library.* *Bottom left:* Bess' mother, Madge Gates Wallace, was often called "The queenliest woman Independence ever produced." *Courtesy Kansas City Star. Bottom right:* David Willock Wallace, father of Bess, was extremely popular and led town parades astride his large white horse. *Courtesy Harry S. Truman Library.*

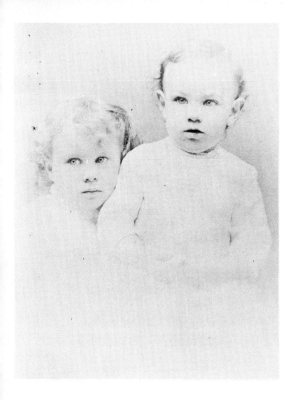

Above: Four-year-old Bess Wallace and her brother Frank, age two. *Courtesy Harry S. Truman Library.* *Right:* Harry Truman at age four with his younger brother Vivian. *Thomson Studio, Kansas City, Mo. Courtesy Harry S. Truman Library.*

Above: Bess as teenage belle and tomboy. *Courtesy Harry S. Truman Library. Left:* Harry at fifteen already had a passion for bow ties. *Courtesy Harry S. Truman Library.*

Above: Graduation day, 1901. Bess, 2nd row, far right; Harry, top row, fourth from left. *Courtesy Harry S. Truman Library. Below:* Truman's 1910 convertible stuffed with picnickers Natalie Ott Wallace, Frank Wallace, Bess and Harry. *Courtesy Harry S. Truman Library.*

Above: "Captain Harry," commander of Battery D, 129th Field Artillery, 35th Division, wrote to Bess every day. *Courtesy Harry S. Truman Library. Below:* Harry with three wartime buddies in the Truman and Jacobson Haberdashery, Kansas City, Mo. *The Kansas City Star.*

Wedding, June 28, 1919. Bess wore imported white georgette. The bridegroom wore a black-and-white checkered suit. *Courtesy Harry S. Truman Library.*

Above: Ten-year-old Margaret, County Judge Harry Truman, and Bess were inseparable. Neighbors referred to them as "The Three Musketeers." *The Kansas City Star. Below:* 1940: The three Trumans celebrate Harry's senate victory. *UPI.*

Above: Bess and Margaret at the 1944 Democratic National Convention in Philadelphia. *Wide World Photos. Right:* Actress Lauren Bacall and the new Vice-President entertain at the National Press Club. *UPI.*

Above: Two and a half hours after Roosevelt's death a grief-stricken Bess listens to Chief Justice Harlan Stone swear Harry in as President. *The Washington Star. Below:* Bess (center) invited her Independence Tuesday Bridge Club to Washington. *Wide World Photos.*

Bess photographed poorly, loathed the camera, but felt this was one of her better ones. *Courtesy Harry S. Truman Library.*

Right: Bess and Margaret arrive at the Capitol to hear the President's fourth State of the Nation message, January 5, 1949. *Wide World Photos. Below:* First Lady Bess Truman opened the March of Dimes campaign by dropping coins into a bottle, then treated all the children to chocolate ice cream cones. *The New York Times.*

Above: The Trumans entertain the future Queen Elizabeth and her husband, Prince Philip, in Washington. *Historical Pictures Services, Inc. Below:* Clifton Daniel, Jr., and Margaret emerge from the Truman home in Independence shortly before their wedding. *Wide World Photos.*

Above: Harry and Bess arrive at Le Havre aboard liner *United States* for seven-week tour of Europe. *Wide World Photos. Below:* The Churchill family welcomes Harry and Bess, American tourists. *Wide World Photos.*

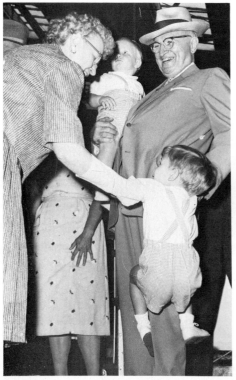

Top left: Clifton Truman Daniel, 3, ask "Grammy" to lift him up as "Dad Grampa" holds one-year-old William Wallace Daniel *Wide World Photos. Above:* Bess, always a avid baseball fan, marks her scoreboard at Boston/Kansas City game. *Wide World Photos Left:* Independence, Mo.: President Lyndo Johnson signs the Medicare Bill in Bess' presence. "The Trumans did a lot to make possible," he said. *Wide World Photos.*

Above: Bess, 84, and Harry, 85, on the back porch of their home. The former President told reporters, "For me she still has the golden curls of yesteryear." *Courtesy Harry S. Truman Library. Right:* Harry died on December 26, 1972. A solemn but composed Bess accepts the flag that had been draped over President Truman's coffin as her daughter and son-in-law look on. *Independence Examiner.*

Above: Harry's Lamar, Mo., birthplace, a modest home for no-nonsense people. *Courtesy Missouri Department of Natural Resources. Below:* 219 North Delaware, Bess' birthplace and where, she says, "I hope to die." *Independence Examiner.*

coaxing she reluctantly agreed to answer questions submitted in writing:

Q: What qualities, innate or acquired, does she think would be the greatest asset of the wife of a President?
A: Good health and a well-developed sense of humor.
Q: Does she think there will ever be a woman President of the United States.
A: No.
Q: Would she want to be President?
A: No.
Q: Does she keep a scrapbook of her husband's activities?
A: No.
Q: Of Margaret's?
A: Yes.
Q: Does she keep a diary?
A: No.
Q: Does unfavorable criticism of the President disturb her?
A: After twenty-five years in politics, she has learned to accept it to a certain extent.
Q: What is her reaction to musical criticism of Margaret's singing?
A: No comment.
Q: Has she discovered any ways of sparing herself during such tasks as receiving of guests?
A: So far I have not felt it a task.
Q: Will you go to the Democratic National Convention in '48?
A: I wouldn't miss a Democratic Convention if I could help it.
Q: If you had a son would you try to bring him up to be President?
A: No.
Q: What would you like to do when your husband is no longer President?
A: Return to Independence, Missouri.

There was little doubt that Bess fervently wanted to go home. People close to her knew that she was trying desperately to dissuade Harry from running. "The President's job is a thankless one," she told Mrs. Vinson. "He takes the blame for every single thing . . . Harry has served the country long enough."

At the time labor leaders and New Dealers were loudly blaming Truman for the war in Korea, rising prices, and shortages. They were defecting by the dozens. Some party kingpins made no secret about wanting to dump the President and draft Eisenhower.

"That's when Bess wavered," said Ethel Noland. "She didn't want Harry to run, but she honestly believed the voters needed him because he was the only candidate who could possibly lead the country into peace and prosperity."

Having secured his wife's blessing, Truman announced that he was a candidate. When Bess and Harry arrived in Philadelphia to attend the Democratic Convention, many of the delegates turned the *W* around and greeted the Trumans with placards that read: "I'm Just *M*ild About Harry."

Columnist Drew Pearson promptly predicted that Truman had about one chance in a thousand of being successful. "All Harry needs is one chance," Bess said. "It will be an uphill fight, but we're used to that. When it's over, Harry will be declared the victor!"

XV THE INCREDIBLE '48 CAMPAIGN

IN THE NEARLY two hundred years of the country's Presidential history, there has been no campaign comparable to the one Truman waged in 1948 against New York Governor Thomas E. Dewey, the Republican candidate for President; Henry A. Wallace, FDR's former Vice-President, running on the Progressive Party ticket; and South Carolina Governor J. Strom Thurmond, who headed the States' Rights Party, commonly referred to as Dixiecrats.

At the more than 350 rallies that attracted 12 million people, Harry, vigorous, cool, confident, didn't often deign to answer charges or counter the promises of his opponents. He was a new "happy warrior" in the Al Smith tradition. He did not wear FDR's mantle, the aristocratic cape, but his own scrubby overcoat, which plainly showed where Bess's skillful darning reinforced the buttons. (Richard Nixon once said that idea of mentioning his wife's "cloth" coat, which he used so effectively in his Checkers speech, came directly from Truman's "common man" wardrobe.)

And there were his two backup stars, Bess and daughter Margaret, exhibiting plainness, simplicity, practicality and, yes, honesty. "The Truman family is typical USA," was the image the three projected.

The Ferdinand Magellan, the specially built Pullman the government had purchased for a dollar from the Association of American Railroads, carried the First Family thirty thousand miles and was home to them for seven weeks. "Bess tried hard to make it liveable," said Charlie Ross. "She saw that it was always clean and neat. But still she realized that it was only a railroad car."

It contained a lounge, a dining area, four staterooms, a galley and a bathroom. The car directly in front was filled with Secret Servicemen, and the fifteen other cars carried reporters, radio correspondents, photographers, clerical help, staff men, servants and some local VIPs who hopped aboard for brief appearances before home-town audiences.

At every whistle-stop—often fifteen a day—the President would wind up his off-the-cuff "Give 'em hell, Harry" speeches with a flash of an infectious smile and a knowing wink, as though he were offering a special treat. Then he would ask the crowd that was packed against the Ferdinand Magellan's rear platform, "Howja like to meet my family?"

Amid loud hoorays, he'd raise both hands and announce joyfully, "Here comes the boss." Bess would appear, waving good-humoredly in response to the noisy welcome, and take her place on his right side. Then the President would invariably say, "Now here's the one who bosses the boss." Margaret would join her mother and father from behind the dark blue velvet curtains that shielded the Pullman's back door.

For her there would also be cheers, plus a few wolf calls and cries of "Give us a song!" Then with the local high school band or its equivalent blaring the "Missouri Waltz," the train would slowly pull away. Bess said recently, "It was probably the last real whistle-stopping campaign we'll ever see."

This scene had dignity, it had warmth, and it put the nation's First Family on a comfortable footing with millions of Americans whose own home family life was reflected there. "They reasoned," said Victor Messall, Truman's former senate secretary who had become part of the Presidential inner circle, "'Here are some plain folks like ourselves that we can believe and trust.' The fact that Truman often inflicted damage to the English language—a few *ain'ts, you was* instead of *you were,* some *hells* and *damns*—only endeared him to them."

They would often present the Trumans with baskets of apples, ears of corn, homegrown peaches. In Chariton, Iowa, one well-wishing farmer wanted to show his support by giving them a week-old piglet. Bess graciously accepted the gifts—all but the piglet. She told the farmer that it wouldn't be fair to keep it on the train. "Tell you what," she said. "When it's of age, smoke it and invite us to dinner."

At a Dexter, Iowa, rally, Bess walked over to Harry and shifted a red carnation from his right to his left lapel. The small, wifely gesture raised a cheer. The next day a local newspaper ran a story and photo about this performance. The caption read: "Bess showed she's one of us."

The First Lady's role in the long, hard campaign was then considerably more than that of tactful hostess and visible spouse. "If you ask me, the whole notion for the trip came from her," Messall said. "She would often tell Harry to run the way he did when he was campaigning for county judge."

Bess sat in on most of the policy-making sessions and offered suggestions that Truman constantly included in his speeches. In addition she served as a one-woman Gallup poll and audience-reaction tester, keeping a sharp eye and ear on the crowds which listened to her husband's oratory. She was also the careful censor of the President's occasional lapses toward overexuberance, halting attempts to hurl his hat into the crowd or dance the Missouri Waltz.

She'd say, "Harry, you've got only one hat. Remember, you're not as rich as Tom Dewey." And, "Jigging isn't dignified."

Just outside Akron, Ohio, Truman told Daniel Seitzman,

a campaign worker, "She has her head filled with smart old-fashioned, good-humored common sense. She is never devious. She knows exactly what people need and want to hear and what they are worried about. She sees that I give it to them standing face to face with no two-dollar words—she's dead set against my using them." Then he added with his impish little-boy grin, "When she thinks I'm getting too big for my britches, she puts me on a diet of humble pie."

In Shelbyville, Kentucky, the press expected fireworks when Truman told a story of how his grandfather Anderson Shippe had run off with a local farm girl. The young lady's mother was so furious that she refused to sanction the union. Fearing her parents' wrath, the couple moved to Missouri. It wasn't until four years later when the in-laws were anxious to see their new grandchild that they effected a reconciliation.

The President then lowered his voice and said, "Confidentially, I've come to Shelbyville to see if my grandparents were ever legally married." The crowd was delighted, but reporters were sure Bess wouldn't approve. They were wrong. She smiled when she heard about it and said, "That Harry! Sometimes I just can't stop him." Nevertheless, she dispatched an aide to make the rounds of the press cars and assure the journalists that they had just listened to one of Truman's "fanciful tales."

As a rule, Bess didn't like the in-law jokes Truman loved to tell. In Helper, Utah, the crowd roared when he compared the Republican Party to "big-mouthed mother-in-laws who get all burnt up because they aren't invited to some *kaffeeklatch.*" He explained that he meant they were kept out because only the Democrats had an easy fellowship with farmers and blue-collar workers.

"When Harry got back to his private car," Ross said, "Bess laid down the law to him. He never gave out with a mother-in-law joke again, but she never knew what to expect from him next."

In Ardmore, Oklahoma, Harry opened a horse's mouth and peered at the animal's teeth. "Six years old," he cried.

"Correct," said the horse's owner.

At which point a reporter heard Bess say, "Perhaps he should use the same method with the grandchildren of our friends. He's forever confusing their ages."

On Saturday, September 26, 1948, the Trumans stopped in Uvalde, Texas, to see seventy-nine-year-old John Nance Garner, FDR's first Vice-President. Garner fed them a "typical" Texas breakfast: white wing dove, smoked ham, bacon, fried chicken, scrambled eggs, rice in gravy, hot biscuits, honey, peach preserves, grape jelly, coffee, and buttermilk.

At the conclusion of the lavish meal, Harry presented his host with a sizeable black satchel. "Here's some medicine for snakebites," he said. It contained a dozen bottles of carefully aged Kentucky bourbon.

The crowd that had gathered before dawn to watch the Trumans enter Garner's house were still there when they emerged several hours later. Bess was so moved that she broke her usual public silence and said, "Thank you from the bottom of my heart for your wonderful tribute and the fact that you came out at the incredible hour of 5 A.M."

She wasn't that pleasant a few days later in Waco, Texas, when her husband was booed for shaking hands with a black woman. In a stage whisper that was heard clearly ten feet away, she said, "Don't mind them, Harry! You did the right thing!"

Bess emphasized her point just as the Ferdinand Magellan was pulling out. She noticed a little black girl seated in a wheelchair. She waved to her. The pleased child waved back. This time people applauded.

Bess was also busy behind the scenes. If the President showed signs of strain, it was she who ordered him to rest. If his voice became hoarse from the ceaseless speech making, she swabbed his throat with a mixture of glycerin and lemon. Without making speeches or holding press conferences, she had become an essential part of her husband's drawing power and an invaluable asset in his drive for election.

"Dewey tried to copy Truman's whistle-stopping," Messall said. "But for him it didn't work so well."

The Republican candidate made a bagful of errors. The worst was in Beaucoup, Illinois, when he was speaking to a crowd from his train platform. Suddenly the locomotive started backing the train toward the crowd. Fortunately it stopped just in time. Although there was alarmed scrambling, no one was injured, but Dewey blew his own stack. "That's the first lunatic I've had for an engineer!" the rattled candidate spluttered. "He probably should be shot at sunrise, but we'll let him off this time since no one was hurt!"

"Bess agreed with speech writers Clark Clifford and Charles Murphy that Harry make something of the incident," recalled Messall. "For the next week Harry'd say, 'We've been hearing about engineers from the Republican candidate. He objects to having engineers back up. He doesn't mention that under that great engineer, Herbert Hoover, we backed up into the worst depression in our history.'"

The tremendous turnouts encouraged Truman supporters. But still most newspapers and periodicals were predicting a solid Republican victory. The politically active left-wing support of Henry Wallace's third party was expected to siphon off as many as five million votes from the Democrats. Hep southern Democrats prophesied that Thurmond's Dixiecrats would have similar success below the Mason-Dixon Line.

The *New York Times* said that Dewey was a certain shoo-in. Its political experts forecast that the Republican candidate would compile 345 electoral votes, to 105 for Truman.

The Detroit *Free Press* urged Truman to start acting like a statesman in his remaining eighty-six days as President and fire his secretary of state. In his place, the newspaper advised, appoint John Foster Dulles, Dewey's certain choice for the job—"So that Dulles could get a flying start."

The November 1, 1948, issue of *Life* magazine ran a long story about the clever strategy with which the Republican candidate was already trouncing poor Truman. They wound up the eight-page feature with a picture of Dewey, captioned: "The next President travels by ferry boat over the broad waters of San Francisco Bay."

Bess looked at the photograph and said wryly, "The man who wrote that caption is certainly going to be embarrassed. I hope he doesn't get fired."

When the vote counting had been completed, Truman had 24,105,812 to Dewey's 21,970,065.* That was despite the fact that the candidates of both the Progressive and States' Rights parties had each polled a million votes, which would have normally gone to the Democrats.

On the Trumans' return to Washington from Independence, where they had voted, Harry, at the urging of press photographers, gleefully held up a copy of the Chicago *Daily Tribune,* which bore a premature headline: "DEWEY DEFEATS TRUMAN." Bess usually curbed her husband's friskiness. This time she had handed him the newspaper.

---

* Once I told the First Lady that my father had predicted Truman would win by 2 million votes. "Your father must be a wise man," she said. *"Life* should have employed him."

XVI NO LONGER AN ERSATZ TENANT

BESS HAD BEEN described by Clare Boothe Luce as "the ersatz First Lady who accidentally stumbled into the White House." The congresswoman-writer went on to say that Mrs. Truman was only a squatter in the Executive Mansion, and that no one ever sent her an engraved invitation.

Shortly after Harry had been elected on his own merit, Bess told Ethel Noland, "Now I guess we've been invited by some twenty-four million Americans. Even to the likes of Mrs. Luce, I should appear genuine." Miss Noland felt that the congresswoman's unkind statement had disturbed Bess more than usual, and she frowningly considered sending her a notarized copy of the final vote count.

"True to form, Clare was totally wrong," said press secretary Charlie Ross. "Everyone who really knows Bess is very aware that she is solid 14-K. The times she's away from Washington you still get the feeling that she's indeed a bona fide First Lady. Not that she's pretentious or displays royal stateliness, but there is always a certain quiet distinction of the White House surrounding her."

Several days after the '48 election, the Trumans went to Key West, Florida, for a vacation. Reporters who usually covered the President decided to stage a parade honoring his spectacular triumph. They decked themselves out in ridiculous-looking costumes and marched in review past Harry and his family. Bess laughed the hardest when Ross appeared in a pair of red-white-and-blue swimming trunks plus a very high Abraham Lincoln stovepipe hat.

"If you had only worn that outfit when we were back in school," she told him. "I'm sure that in addition to your being the smartest boy in our class, you'd have also been voted the best dressed."

To a journalist who was wearing a bed sheet, she said, "You now look like a ghost writer."

Ross recalled, "Bess really enjoyed our silly shenanigans, but even then her laugh, which was hearty, sounded ladylike. I know it may sound inconsistent. It is something wonderful to hear. Comes from deep down, rises upward, and then bubbles forth. Margaret inherited that quality."

After a two-week holiday the Trumans returned to Washington, where they learned that they would have to vacate the White House because it was literally falling apart. The President's bathtub was sinking into the ceiling of the Red Room, one leg of Margaret's piano had already gone through the floor, and the lamps in Bess's bedroom lurched dangerously.

"When we left," she said, "they swayed when I walked in sort of a slow Stephen Foster tempo. Now the beat was much more violent, like that of George Gershwin's *Rhapsody in Blue.*"

In the 180 years since President John Adams first took up residence in the White House, pinch-penny Congress had voted very small sums for physical maintenance and repairs. The result was what architects called a near-fatality. A

commission was appointed to study the badly ailing building. After great deliberation they presented three possible
solutions:

> 1. Tear down the existing structure and try to
> re-create it with as much old material as possible.
> 2. Destroy the building and erect a brand new
> White House, keeping the same design.
> 3. Preserve the outer walls, gut the interior and
> rebuild it using original materials where possible,
> exact reproductions where not.

"Most people think it was only Harry who had a deep
sense of history," said Snyder. "It's also Bess. She takes
great pride in time-honored American institutions. Especially the White House. The country should be eternally
grateful to her for the persuasive part she played in keeping
it in one piece."

She strongly favored the third suggestion. Congress
wanted to construct a brand new Executive Mansion, since
it would be cheaper than trying to restore the old one. That
was when Bess decided that some heavy lobbying was
necessary. She buttonholed influential senators and repre-
sentatives. "She pointed out that the public had long
memories," said Sam Rayburn. "And that they would be
forever angry if we abandoned the historic building."

Bess sent a special message to the press, saying that the
White House walls had to be saved. She phoned wives of
Washington bigwigs whom she felt might help. Mrs. Robert
Taft, whose husband, the senior senator from Ohio, was
often referred to as Mr. Republican, said, "Browbeating
was not her style, but she let it be known that the building
had to be saved at all costs. No—not had to be saved—was
going to be saved!"

The First Lady won her point. Ultimately Congress

agreed to appropriate $5.4 million for complete renovation of the White House. It was the most costly and most thorough face-lifting job ever undertaken on any national edifice. However, it meant that the Trumans would once again have to live in Blair House—this time for several years. Residing there would present serious problems— Blair House simply wasn't big enough.

To help solve the difficulty, Blair House was joined with the adjacent building, Lee House. Doors were cut through on each floor. Still the combined area wasn't sufficient to entertain properly, and it was decided to use nearby hotels for huge affairs and to depend on a series of small receptions at home. Bess didn't mind the arrangements and said philosophically, "People get to know each other much better at intimate functions."

By the beginning of 1949, the Trumans were comfortably settled in the temporary Executive Mansion. That was when a rumor circulated that the First Lady was a secret patient in the University of Iowa Hospital. Get-well cards by the hundreds poured in. It turned out to be another Mrs. Harry Truman from Tipton, Iowa.

"I sincerely hope my namesake gets well soon," said the authentic wife of the President. "But definitely, I'm not in the hospital. However, there are times I wish I were there until the day after the inauguration on January twentieth!"

Great preparations were made for that day. It began at 7 A.M. with breakfast at the Mayflower Hotel for ninety-eight former members of Battery D, which Truman had commanded in World War I. The exuberant veterans presented Harry with a gold-headed cane. One of them later said to Bess, "We'd appreciate your seeing to it that the captain uses it on his early morning walks."

Bess replied firmly, "I'll see to it!" She laughed as she added, "If he doesn't, I'll give him a good whack with it."

Following breakfast, Bess, Harry and Margaret attended services at St. John's Episcopal Church. Then they returned

to Blair House to wait for a joint congressional committee
to escort them to the Capitol for the swearing-in ceremony
of Harry and the new Vice-President, Alben Barkley.

"Captain Harry stood every bit as he did in France," said
Eddie Meisenburger, a veteran of Battery D. "His lady
looked on proudly. I could see her eyes were wet."

This time Bess's eyes glistened with happiness as she
watched her husband raise his right hand, place his left hand
on the Bible and take the oath of office. She told Ethel
Noland, "He was every inch a President in his striped pants,
black morning coat and high silk hat. My, what a job to get
him into it! His inaugural address, in which he listed a four-
point program for our foreign policy, was one of the most
distinguished speeches I ever heard. There were thirteen
bursts of applause."

After a quick lunch the Trumans participated in a long
parade down Pennsylvania Avenue, with the men from
Battery D serving as an honor guard. As one of them ran
alongside, Bess said, "It's cold. Button your coat!"

Then in the frigid January weather Bess sat in the
reviewing stand for three and a half hours. She thanked a
delegation from Massachusetts when they presented her
with a bouquet of roses. She vigorously applauded the West
Point cadets, Annapolis midshipmen, pretty drum major-
ettes and Missouri mules. She waved individually at hundreds of dignitaries, but kept her arms firmly folded when J.
Strom Thurmond, the defeated Dixiecrat candidate for
President, rode by as part of the South Carolina delegation.
Instead she turned her head in the direction of actress
Tallulah Bankhead, who loudly booed the racist governor.

"I wish I had nerve enough to do that," she whispered to
a friend sitting near her.

When one woman waved a placard which read, "Even
Iowa voted Democratic," Bess tossed her a flower. The
First Lady had to leave before the parade was over so that
she could dress for a reception at the National Gallery.

There she heard Harry and Barkley each give the same speech twice because the audience was so vast that two rooms had to be used.

The Trumans then returned to Blair House for a late dinner and for more clothes-changing. Bess wore a sedate black velvet gown to the Inaugural Ball, which was held at the National Guard Armory. Ten thousand people tried to crowd into space that had been intended for less than half that number. Couples stood so closely together they could only sway to the music of band leaders Benny Goodman, Guy Lombardo and Xavier Cugat. Bess, who was sitting in the Presidential box, witnessed the confusion and said to Harry, "The way they are moving about even you could dance!"

At 2:20 A.M. a very weary First Lady, who had been on center stage for more than nineteen hours, was finally allowed to go to sleep. As she was about to close the door to her bedroom in Blair House, she said wearily, "I wonder if Martha Washington's feet ached so much."

XVII THE PRESIDENT'S MOTHER-IN-LAW

BESS AND HARRY shared living quarters with Madge Wallace for many years. During that period they frequently heard her mutter, "My daughter could have married someone from her own background!"

"She seemed to delight in belittling her son-in-law," said Ethel Noland. "Even when Harry became President, she continued to put him down. She was never sold on the idea that he was qualified to do anything properly. And she wasn't at all reserved in talking about it. She'd say things like, 'I know dozens of men better qualified to be in Mr. Truman's place in the White House!'

"I'm sure it caused Harry a great deal of distress, but you never caught him making a single negative statement against her in any fashion. The nearest he came is when once he kidded, 'I wonder if Madge Wallace is related to Henry Wallace?'"

Miss Noland had other thoughts about Truman and his mother-in-law. "Being browbeaten by her," she said, "only endeared him and made him seem more human to people close by. Some new acquaintances once hazarded charitably that the aging woman was getting senile. Harry replied cheerily, 'Oh, my, she's always like that. But any fellow who married her Bess would have got the same treatment.'"

Despite Truman's unfailing considerateness toward his spouse, the First Lady had to walk a very thin rope when the situation revolved around her husband and her mother. No incident was too trivial to provoke absurd caustic comment from Mrs. Wallace. Of her tolerant son-in-law she remarked loudly that he didn't comb his hair properly, that his bow tie wasn't appropriate, that he made too much noise when swallowing soup and sipped it off the wrong part of the spoon.

Bess carefully tried to avoid antagonistic answers. However, the day after Truman dismissed General Douglas MacArthur for insubordination, the servants heard Mrs. Wallace peevishly ask her daughter, "Why did your husband have to fire that nice man? Why didn't he let General MacArthur run the Korean War in his own way? Imagine a captain from the National Guard telling off a West Point general!"

This time Bess snapped back belligerently, "My husband, Mother, happens to be commander-in-chief! And that outranks a general! My husband does what he believes best for the country!" Then she turned her back on her mother and marched out of the room. It was very rare for Bess to make any hostile reply, and a few minutes later she returned to apologize.

Bess insisted on personally caring for Mrs. Wallace and seemed to ignore the fact that it complicated her life to a point where another woman would blow up. Her brother Fred said, "She always was a devoted daughter. She saw to it that my mother didn't lack for anything. Why, my mother's room has every possible comfort. Bess is a very thoughtful daughter.''

In later years Mrs. Wallace seldom left that room. Each day Bess spent time with her. "She really loved that lady,'' recalled Mrs. Parks, "although at times I think she found her childishly annoying. One day the First Lady had an extra heavy schedule and had to cut her visit short. You would have thought the world was coming to an end the way Mrs. Wallace carried on. Her way of getting back was to refuse to eat.''

That was when one of Bess's friends offered to help. She said that her mother had presented a similar problem, and she successfully solved it by using a combination of firmness and tact. The following day the well-meaning woman, to demonstrate her sweet persuasion, entered Mrs. Wallace's room and in a determined, singsong voice, cooed, "Eat all that food like my good little girl!''

Again Mrs. Wallace turned thumbs down. This time she said haughtily, "I'll have you know that *I'm not your good little girl! Now, I want to take a nap so do please leave the room!*'' The visitor scuttled.

When the President heard about the incident, he was amused. "Here I thought Bess inherited her sense of humor from her father,'' he said delightedly. "I see that it comes from her mother, too.''

Once when Bess was visiting Margaret in New York, Harry tried to pinch-hit for his wife. Lillian Rogers Parks recalled that occasion. "Mrs. Wallace didn't exactly welcome his entering her room. When he stopped by to see how she was getting on, she'd lean over and pretend to pick something up or put something away in a drawer. She'd make out that she didn't see or hear him. She was not going to be egged into saying so much as good morning to that man if she didn't have to! I mentioned it to Mr. Prettyman, the President's valet, and he explained it this way: 'Mrs. Wallace always thought Harry Truman wouldn't amount to anything. It galls her to see him in the White House ruining that prediction.'"

Some White House employees were convinced that Mrs. Wallace suffered from a plain case of jealousy where Harry was concerned. "It irritated her badly to see the President and Mrs. Truman together," said one. "Whenever that happened, she would try anything to pry them apart. When she was still well enough to come down to meals, I remember one time she saw the President escort Bess to a seat at the table and then place his hand on his wife's hair in a loving, caressing pat. Mrs. Wallace saw red when she caught that gesture. Her hands shook so that she knocked over a pitcher of cream. Whether it was an accident or done on purpose to distract them, I can't say, but the cream dripped down on Bess's dress and the President got even closer to his wife, trying to mop it up. The old lady got even madder than ever. 'Ask the maid to do that!' she snapped.

"'Aw, it's my pleasure,' the President said and grinned. He was on to her, you see."

Margaret, on the other hand, found her grandmother to be "a gentle-looking woman who always seemed interested in my welfare." She said, "When I was a child, my Grandmother Wallace would give me cookies and see to it that my friends and I had sufficient money for the movies. As I grew older, she was pleased with my successes."

At the age of ninety Madge Wallace suffered a severe stroke. A week later she died of cerebral thrombosis. Her body was taken to Independence for burial. Ethel Noland, who was one of the mourners, said, "I suppose in some ways she was a mystery. But in spite of whatever faults Mrs. Wallace possessed, she had good qualities, too. After all, wasn't she the mother of Bess Truman?"

Some Truman friends have quietly speculated that Bess's enigmatic relationship with her mother was not such a mystery after all. It would have been "so sensible" for her

to give her mother into the care of one of her brothers, who
had repeatedly volunteered for the job. Why, then, did she
not? There is no record that Mrs. Wallace expressed a wish,
one way or the other.

One intimate said, "Don't use my name—the family
would boil me in oil—but I think Bess got some comfort
from making her mother live each day with the overwhelming triumph of Harry Truman, the man Madge Wallace had
sneeringly predicted would amount to nothing. And perhaps it was a bit of vengeance, too, for the memory of her
father, who had taken his own life because he could not live
up to the demanding expectations of his wife.

"Bess loved those two men with all her heart."

XVIII GOOD QUEEN BESS

DURING TRUMAN'S SECOND term, newspaper correspondents covering the Washington scene began to treat Bess, as First Lady, with more respect and deference. Drew Pearson, a nationally syndicated columnist who often wrote unflattering stories about the President, said, "She has become one of the most influential people around—probably the most influential with Harry. She is currently his most trustworthy cohort."

Then the journalist, who had been called an S.O.B. by Truman, added, "Her clout, however, rarely shows as she continues to hide her talent under a bushel. If not for her quiet, diplomatic expertise and regal bearing, her husband would be in a lot more hot water than he's presently in."

Walter Lippmann, the noted pundit, also acknowledged her importance to the President. "He's a mighty lucky man to have chosen so wisely," said the dean of Washington newsmen. "She has come to be indispensable to him . . . an ideal associate in every sense."

Bess's nightly conferences with her husband, still a firm domestic habit, seemed to carry more weight than ever.

Insiders said that she was the one who counseled him to fire General MacArthur. Truman himself told a reporter, "The Boss is not only my good right arm, but the left one as well."

In addition to guiding the President, Bess continued to be "honorary chairman" and "distinguished patroness" of programs sponsored by national organizations, among them the Girl Scouts of America, Red Cross, YWCA, American Cancer Society, March of Dimes, Salvation Army, and the ASPCA.

At one meeting of the American Society for the Prevention of Cruelty to Animals, the ever-shy First Lady was called upon to speak. Quaking, she timidly walked up to the podium. "Thank you for asking me here," she said. "I wish you good luck." Then she quicky returned to her seat.

"But she was not content to just sit still, lend her name and be honored," said Edith Helm, her social secretary. "Mrs. Truman would send out reams of letters and make scores of phone calls pleading for help—a real chairman's job. I'm sure she personally raised loads of money."

As First Ladies have done in the past, Bess held receptions for VIPs—but on a much smaller scale. According to custom, the President's wife was expected to entertain at tea the wives of congressmen, plus the wives of assorted army, navy, marine and air force bigwigs, plus women of high social or economic rank. Her problem was complicated by the fact that the White House was closed for repairs and Blair House was too small.

What to do?

She devised a plan that other Presidents' wives still use. To accommodate the more than a thousand on her guest list, she divided it into eight parts and served eight teas, summoning most of the guests in alphabetical order. "This proved to be hugely successful," Bess said, "even though one congressman's wife whose name began with a *W* complained about being invited to the final function instead of the first one. She insisted that I should go by her maiden name, which started with the letter *A*."

A few weeks later Bess encountered another grievance, launching what was afterward known as the Great Pudding Apoplexy. It concerned a recipe for Ozark Pudding, which she had contributed to the *Congressional Club Cookbook.* Mrs. Hazel Williams of Richmond, Virginia, wrote: "I tried making your Ozark Pudding. It didn't turn out properly. As a matter of fact it turned out so terrible that my husband and children refused to eat it. You never did specify how to mix it . . . I'm almost sorry I didn't vote for Dewey."

The letter from Mrs. Williams leaked out, and a great controversy arose. Finally, food specialists at the Bureau of Human Nutrition and Home Economics of the Department of Agriculture decided to settle the dispute. After a series of tests a spokesman reported, "There is no right or wrong way. You can either stir or mix with a modern mixing machine, a beat-up wire whisk, or a plain old fork."

As soon as their findings had been completed, Bess sent Mrs. Williams a copy and added, "Please try again. I'm confident that this time it will work out just fine. *It better!* We can't have you feeling sorry that you voted for my husband."

Mrs. Truman's Ozark Pudding

1 egg
¾ cup of sugar
3 heaping tablespoons of flour
1¼ teaspoons of baking powder
1 cup cream, whipped
⅛ teaspoon salt
½ cup chopped nuts
½ cup raw chopped apples
1 teaspoon vanilla

Beat egg well and add sugar, beating until light and creamy. Sift flour, baking powder, salt and add to egg mixture; blend well. Fold in apples and nuts; add vanilla. Pour into greased paper-lined dish; bake in a slow oven (325 degrees) for 30 minutes. Serve with whipped cream or ice cream. A little rum adds to the pudding flavor, but is not necessary.

Despite the Department of Agriculture's convincing statement, Bess was downcast, as she had always prided herself on her cooking. She brightened when a Secret Serviceman said that his wife had prepared the pudding for him. "It was the best dessert I ever ate!" he told the First Lady. "And I must say I'm a judge of desserts!"

Although Bess resented their necessary intrusion, she was on extremely good terms with many members of the Secret Service. One agent said, "I don't dare tell Mrs. Truman when my missus is sick. She'd rush right over to my house and take full charge—even change the baby's diapers. She's not happy when she isn't doing something for others."

While there isn't any record of her diaper changing, she once showed up unexpectedly at the house of a Secret Serviceman whose wife was ill and cooked the Thanksgiving turkey. She helped the daughter of another agent get into veterinary school.

"I wanted to send Mrs. Truman a present," said the girl's grateful father. "But I knew she wouldn't hear of it. Everything she did had to be on the up and up—very scrupulously so."

Bess also took great interest in the agents' religious beliefs. She asked one Catholic Secret Serviceman what his creed was on divorce. He was hesitant in replying. Just then the President walked into the room. "On advice of counsel the witness may decline to answer," Truman said. "Separation of church and state."

"Oh, Harry," Bess said irritably. "Must you have advice for everybody?"

She got even more perturbed when the gift to her of a $375 deep-freeze unit from Truman's chief military aide, General Vaughan, caused loud criticism. Vaughan had received the appliance from a Chicago firm interested in government contracts. "How could I know?" asked Bess indignantly.

She was startled by all the disapproval leveled against her for accepting the freezer. She was even more thunderstruck when a strange ally came to her defense—Senator Joseph McCarthy, who claimed Truman had started the Korean War for "publicity purposes." McCarthy, a Republican member of the subcommittee investigating the influence peddling, said, "There is nothing in the record even remotely suggesting anything improper on the part of Mrs. Truman . . . To her it was no different than accepting several pounds of Wisconsin cheese from an admirer. Just a simple case of proper Midwestern courtesy."

When it had been determined that Bess was blameless, she sadly told Mrs. Vinson, "In the future I'll be very wary of all food freezers and all similar gifts. If someone offers me a tray of ice cubes, I'll refuse it!"

People who knew her intimately weren't at all surprised by McCarthy's statement. "Mrs. Truman is probably the most scrupulous person in all of Missouri," said Albert Bundchus, the owner of a department store in Independence. "One summer in the middle of Harry's second term, she got out of the elevator of our home furnishings floor lugging a folding card table. The manager saw her and quickly offered to carry it for her. She refused, saying that it wasn't heavy. Then she pointed to a tag hanging from one of the legs.

"'It's marked $5.95,' she said. 'Others in the same lot are $6.95.'

"'Well, if it's marked $5.95—that's the price you can have it for,' he said to the President's wife.

"She shook her head. 'There must be a mistake in the

marking,' she insisted. 'It's undamaged. Please check the price for me.'

"There had been an error in the marking. The manager urged her to accept it at the price-tag value. 'No,' she said sternly. 'That wouldn't be honest!'"

When Bess returned to Washington, she enjoyed listening to Margaret practice for an operatic concert she was to give at Constitution Hall. Hours before the scheduled performance Charlie Ross died suddenly of a heart attack. Bess knew how fond her daughter had been of Truman's press secretary and decided not to tell her the bad news until after the concert.

That evening the First Lady and the President heard their daughter sing. They joined the audience in applauding vigorously and demanding an encore. However, the following day their pleasure subsided when a devastating review appeared in the Washington *Post*. Paul Hume, the newspaper's music critic, wrote, "She is flat a good deal of the time. She cannot sing with anything approaching professional finish . . . She communicates almost nothing of the music she presents."

Truman responded immediately. He dashed off a handwritten letter to Hume, which has since become a collector's item. The *Post* published it in its entirety:

> I have just read your lousy review in the back pages. You sound like a frustrated man that never made a success, an eight-ulcer man on a four-ulcer job, and all four ulcers working.
>
> I have never met you, but if I do you'll need a new nose and plenty of beefsteak and perhaps a supporter below. Westbrook Pegler,* a guttersnipe, is a gentleman compared to you. You

*Westbrook Pegler was a prominent conservative journalist who was harshly critical of Truman.

can take that as more of an insult than a reflection
on your ancestry.

When Bess saw the story, she was furious. Perhaps
because of her mother's interference in her own life, the
First Lady strongly believed that children should be permitted to guide their own futures without habitual interference.
She stormed into the Oval Office and loudly berated Harry
for having ruined their daughter's singing career. She said
that he had no business butting into another person's life.

"She sure was burning up with anger," recalled Truman.
"I don't think I've ever seen her so angry."

Bess usually didn't extract promises, but this time she
made her husband give his solemn word of honor that he
would never again send out a personal note to a stranger
concerning his family without discussing it with her be-
forehand.

That afternoon Sam Rayburn called at Blair House. "My
God," he said. "Why doesn't someone hide the pens from
Harry so he can't find them?"

By now Bess was somewhat mollified. "I suppose if we
did that," she replied, "it just wouldn't be Harry. He did a
terrible thing, but I suppose we like him because he's that
way."

However, it was rumored around Washington's National
Press Club that Bess had installed a false bottom on the
mailbox Truman used. And that after he had gone to sleep,
she'd collect his letters, read them carefully and decided
which ones to send out.

"It was very different when the hostile audience started
picking on Harry," Rayburn said. "Instantly she'd rush to
his defense. During normal times she was always nearby,
but during difficult periods it looked as if she never left his
side. She seemed to give him the strength he needed—her
very presence did that. I don't know what her personal
feelings were about his ordering the bombs dropped on

Japan. I do know, however, that after it was done and there were some angry cries, she gave him the love he needed. The strength he needed. I saw it happen over and over."

Morris Ernst, a frequent White House guest whom Truman appointed to the White House Committee on Civil Rights, spoke of other occasions when this was evident. "Joe McCarthy called the President everything in the book," he said. "S.O.B. to traitor. Sometimes it seemed as if Truman would buckle over from the Wisconsin senator's name calling. He didn't, and I credit Bess with that. In the course of those months, I saw them quite often. I'd witness her comforting and soothing him—offering him the consolation and encouragement he so badly required."

The lawyer added, "Harry Truman may have been more liberal politically, but she was definitely the more sympathetic personality. His eye was on the troops. Her eye was on the sparrow. She was his cold towel, brandy and chicken soup all rolled into one."

The most important social event of 1951 came when Princess Elizabeth (now Queen of England) and her husband, the Duke of Edinburgh, stayed at Blair House. Bess took personal charge of their visit. Her ranking public success was the state dinner she arranged. The First Lady selected the menu:

Blue point oysters on half shell
Cocktail sauce, lemon wedges
Crackers
Sherry
Clear soup with marrow balls
Celery hearts   Assorted olives
Melba toast
White wine
Lobster thermidor

Parsleyed sliced tomatoes and cucumbers
Whole wheat bread sandwiches
Red wine
Roast fillet of beef
Wine essence
Watermelon pickles
Broiled mushrooms
French fried potato balls
Asparagus hollandaise
Champagne
Green salad with artichoke hearts
Baked Old Missouri ham
Herb French dressing
Corn sticks
Vanilla ice cream melon molds
Brandied macaroons
Angel food cake

The duke, who could be a bit of a snob, was later overheard to tell his aide, Lieutenant Michael Parker: "For an American, Mrs. Truman did quite well—especially that Missouri ham. I ate so much I had to open a button on my trousers. Perhaps from now on we should refer to her as Good Queen Bess."

XIX DECISION: LEAVE WASHINGTON

SHOULD HE? OR shouldn't he?

The question of whether Truman ought to be a candidate in '52 generated a good deal of heated conversation. The argument became so tense at a reception given by Mrs. Gwendolyn Cafritz (one of the Capitol's superhostesses who regularly gave grand-manner parties for VIPs at her Foxhill estate overlooking the Potomac) that one Southern senator tossed a wineglass at a colleague who disagreed with him.

As the spattered legislator mopped his face, the culprit shouted, "You deserved it for not facing the truth that Truman wants to have his arm twisted! And believe me it won't take much twisting!"

Harry's cousin, Ethel Noland, was amused at the senator's performance when she read about it in the newspaper. "He just didn't know Harry's wife," she said. "Bess was rigidly opposed to the idea of her husband running again. She knew what a man-killer the Presidency was and wanted to keep him alive and well. Why, when Harry came down with a virus infection and was taken to the Walter Reed

Hospital, she didn't let him out of her sight for days. Drove the hospital staff mighty near crazy. Bess knew it would be mainly her decision. In the past Harry had always listened to her and would now. For the time she decided to keep her view quiet, so it was back to business as usual."

On January 9, 1952, the First Lady, who had just returned from a visit to Independence, heard her husband deliver his seventh State of the Union message. Winston Churchill was also in the audience. The colorful British prime minister had come to the United States seeking aid for his country, which was troubled by restless and resentful colonies. Many spectators stared at him instead of listening to the President.

Bess was annoyed. "Harry may not be as silver-tongued as Churchill," she told Alben Barkley. "But I honestly believe the people understand him lots better!"

The Vice-President had come to Blair House for dinner. The seventy-four-year-old Barkley was a widower, and Bess invited him over often because she felt he wasn't eating properly. She was exhilarated when he considered taking the vivacious Jane Hadley of St. Louis as his bride.

He had always put great store in Bess's "practical Midwestern horse sense," and he asked her if she felt a union with a woman forty years his junior was a wise one. She assured him that she approved of his choice.

"She acted the part of Cupid's helper," said Perle Mesta. "She'd have them over and tell each one how nice the other was. If a daughter had resulted from the marriage, I'm sure the thankful couple would have named the baby Bess."

Barkley had once confided to Mrs. Mesta that he hoped Jane would turn out to be as easy to get along with as Bess. "He really admired the First Lady," Mrs. Mesta said. "And Bess liked the Veep because he always was full of the latest gossip. Jolly, harmless gossip, not mean stuff. I remember the time it was about Gwen Cafritz (Perle Mesta and Gwen Cafritz were constantly feuding to be considered the num-

ber-one Washington hostess), who thought she had a hot
scoop about Truman dumping his secretary of interior and
appointing a Mr. Samuel Chichester in his place. Immediately Gwen phoned Mrs. Chichester. 'I hear your husband
is about to be named to the Cabinet,' she said. 'If that's true
please come to dinner on March third. If it's not true come
for coffee later.'

"Bess laughed and laughed. 'That does sound a bit like
her,' she said. 'By the way, I suppose I should tell Harry to
notify Oscar Chapman that he is being replaced—Gwen
Cafritz says so.' In this case both the Veep and the
redoubtable Mrs. Cafritz were mistaken." (Oscar Chapman
served as secretary of the interior from December 1, 1949 to
January 20, 1953.)

Mr. and Mrs. Clark Clifford were another couple the
Trumans frequently entertained. Clifford was one of
Harry's very close aides—Washington journalists said the
closest. Bess was extremely fond of his wife. "Our friendship started when we discovered that we both had played
sandlot baseball as young girls," recalled Mrs. Clifford. "I
think Mrs. Truman used to play third base—I was an
outfielder. She still kept up her interest in the game and was
a wild rooter for the Washington Senators."

Her husband added, "We'd call on them at Blair House
or later at the White House. Sometimes they'd come to see
us. Our times together would usually be family affairs—the
President and my wife might play the piano. He wasn't the
world's best pianist, but you couldn't tell that from Mrs.
Truman's expression. She looked on as if he were another
Paderewski."

On February 13 Bess celebrated her sixty-seventh year
the way she liked best—a quiet dinner at home with Harry.
Blair House servants heard Truman serenade her with
several choruses of "Happy Birthday." "Then there was
total silence," said one of the butlers. "I accidentally

walked into the room the President and Mrs. Truman were in. Luckily they didn't hear me, or they would have been embarrassed—Mrs. Truman more than Harry. She frowned on expressions of sentiment in public. They were sitting side by side on the couch. His right hand was draped around her shoulders and the other was holding one of her hands. Both of them had their eyes closed. I don't think they were sleeping—just looking content. I tiptoed out."

Early in the spring of 1952, the rejuvenation of the White House was declared complete and the Trumans, after living more than three years in Blair House, were allowed to move back in. They were just in time for a visit from Queen Juliana and Prince Bernhard of the Netherlands. The queen remarked, "This time-honored building is truly magnificent. I'm told the plaudits should go to you and President Truman for preserving it."

The First Lady was delighted with her new surroundings and invited female members of the press for a personally guided tour of the living quarters. (The previous day Harry had conducted male correspondents on a similar visit.) "She welcomed us with the pride of any housewife," recalled Lonnelle Aikman, a writer for *National Geographic*. "The innovations were glorious. For the first time in 150 years, White House bedrooms had spacious built-in closets. The most impressive connected the President's bedroom with the First Lady's suite. In the bathroom old fixtures were replaced by gleaming porcelain and metal—with such exotic touches as an eagle etched on the side of the President's bathtub, and a fan on the First Lady's."

Dorothy Kilgallen, a reporter for the Hearst chain of newspapers, also accompanied Bess on the White House inspection tour. She said, "One lady in the party fingered a damask drapery and sighed, 'Oh, Mrs. Truman, what a thrill it must be to live amidst all this beauty and history.'

"Bess turned slightly and gave her a middlewest deadpan

that Grant Wood would have loved. I don't remember her exact quote, so I won't attempt her exact words, but it was the genteel equivalent of 'Nuts!'"

Most of the country's newspapers spoke glowingly of the alterations. Typical was a comment made by a reporter for the Washington *Post:* "The President and the First Lady are to be congratulated on a job well done."

Their architectural proposals hadn't always been treated with such respect. When Harry wanted to build a balcony on the South Portico of the White House, a nationwide hullaballoo resulted. Ethel Noland said, "It seems that it was only after Bess pointed out to Harry—and he to the nation—that it would save the country $1500 a year in awning costs and also function as a fire escape, that the $10,000 balcony was grudgingly accepted."

Several days after the Trumans had once again taken up residence in the White House, they decided the time had come for Harry to inform the nation of his decision about running. He was to be the principal speaker at the Jefferson–Jackson Day Dinner at the Washington Armory. At the end of his address, he said, "I shall not be a candidate for reelection. I have served my country long and I think efficiently and honestly. I shall not accept a renomination. I do not feel that it is my duty to spend another four years in the White House."

There were deep gasps from the audience. "They were stunned," recalled Sam Rayburn. "Couldn't believe what they just heard. When Harry finished, he looked directly at Bess, who was sitting near the podium. He nodded at her as if to say, 'Well, I did it!' She looked both happy and proud. There was the tiniest smile on her lips as if to say, 'No, I did it!'"

John Snyder also saw her that evening. "I could tell that she was relieved that Harry had publicly released the news," he said. "Until that moment she thought he might try to convince her that he was the only possible candidate who could win. But he hadn't. Suddenly her step grew lighter. It was so obvious to see how satisfied she was that at last she would be leaving permanently for Independence."

Then Snyder added, "For the remaining ten months she was an ideal First Lady and did everything that was expected of her. I'd say more. She took care of the President. Advised him. Entertained. Showed off the White House. Headed all sorts of committees. Specify it and she did it."

It ended on January 20, 1953, when Dwight Eisenhower was sworn in. "When I think of that episode," said Rayburn, "I get the jitters. On the morning of the inauguration, Ike refused to get out of his car to fetch Harry to accompany him to the Capitol. That was the way it had always been done—the President-elect would go into the White House and greet the outgoing President and his family. Ike refused. Harry was so infuriated at Ike's behavior that he wanted to go in separate cars. Bess, God bless her, saved the day. She pointed out that another person's bad manners didn't mean that you had to act likewise. Harry eventually came out to Eisenhower's waiting car and climbed in."

The soon-to-be-replaced First Lady heard the Marine Band play "Hail to the Chief" to her husband for the final time as he took his place on the inaugural stand. She heard the song again as he walked down the unpainted raw wood steps at the rear of the platform. But this time it was for President Eisenhower. Bess made a gesture to open her purse, possibly for a handkerchief to wipe her eyes. Instead she joined Harry and together they left the Capitol in a closed car.

Shortly after the inauguration ceremony Bess and Harry had lunch at Dean Acheson's house in old Georgetown, where they received a tumultuous ovation. The luncheon was attended by the entire cabinet, ex-cabinet members and

White House aides. Bess shook hands with all of them. "This is probably the last time I'll ever have to stand in a receiving line," she told Acheson. "Just when I've learned how to do it without hurting. You flex your knees and put your weight on the outside of your feet. I should tell Mrs. Eisenhower about it."

At 6 P.M. the now-private citizens Bess and Harry Truman left for Washington's Union Station to board a train to Independence. As the train pulled out, a throng of about five thousand people broke into "Auld Lang Syne." There were several homemade signs. One said, "Goodbye Darby and Joan.* A long and happy life. You made families count once again."

*Darby and Joan were a loving husband and wife said to have lived in perfect harmony, who were made famous by an eighteenth century popular ballad: "The Happy Old Couple."

XX RETURN TO INDEPENDENCE

MORE THAN TEN thousand men, women and children, almost a fourth of Independence's population in 1953, greeted the Trumans when their train pulled in. Randall Jessee, news director for station WDAF in Kansas City, covered their arrival. "I have never seen such a frenzied welcome," he recalled. "The people—all of them considered themselves their neighbors—were beside themselves. I had thought that at best a few hundred would show up. Diehards. After all, we had just finished a red-hot campaign and the Truman program seemed soundly repudiated by the vote for Eisenhower.

"Bess was so moved by the reception and so glad to be home that she grasped a microphone that was handed to her instead of pushing it away as she usually did, and started to speak. However, she was too choked up to say much. The crowd understood and there was more yelling mixed with tears. People were laughing, whistling and crying at the same time. It was a sight I'll never forget. I remember Harry saying to her, 'Bess, they sure must love you.'"

When the Trumans got to 219 North Delaware Street,

there was another huge crowd waiting. By this time the former First Lady had regained her composure. As they entered the house, she said, "If this is what you get for all those years of hard work, I suppose it was worth it." Then she added, "Harry, the minute we get unpacked, you carry the suitcases up to the attic! That will prove we're home at last for good!"

Now that the neighbors had demonstrated their hearts' feelings, they decided that the Trumans needed some quiet to get readjusted to their old routine. "Not so with outsiders," John Snyder said. "The phone began ringing at once. Lots of calls were job offers: the chairmanship of several big companies—a sewing machine company, a railroad, a clothing store chain, a movie company. All had six-figure salaries and a few hours of work. He and Bess saw through them right away; it wasn't Harry Truman they were interested in, but the prestige of the ex-President!"

One of the first things the Trumans did on their return home was to drive over to the Independence library. There were no more Secret Servicemen to bother them, and Harry did the chauffeuring. Mrs. Vinson had recommended a novel that she had enjoyed reading. Bess was eager to take it out. While Harry remained in the car, she went in and walked over to the stacks. Miss Ethel Tiffy, the head librarian, rushed over and offered to help. "No, thank you," Bess said resolutely. "My eyes may be somewhat weaker, but they still function. If you don't mind I'll do my own looking. Besides you must have more important things to do."

The word soon got out that the Trumans wanted to be left alone. Even Bess's bridge-club friends were reluctant to disturb them. That was when Randall Jessee decided that they must be lonely. "I think people just are afraid to invite them out," he told his wife Fern. "I'll find out if they'll come to our house for dinner."

The next day he asked Harry. "I'm sure we'd like to,"

Truman replied. "Let me check with the boss." Fern Jessee promptly received an affirmative note from Bess. Soon the Trumans were dining out at least once a week.

"On one of their visits to our house," said Jessee, "an incident occurred that convinced me how down-to-earth Mrs. Truman really was. She asked my wife where the bathroom was. We had an old house and it was tucked away underneath the stairway. It had a pull-chain light located in an obscure place. Fern went in ahead of Mrs. Truman to turn it on. She was flabbergasted when she suddenly saw the President standing there.

"'I had to go and couldn't find the light,' the former President said sheepishly.

"Fern apologized for the intrusion and tried to back out. That was when Mrs. Truman said, 'Harry, weren't you about through anyway?'"

In the summer of '53 the Trumans decided to drive to Washington, and from there to Philadelphia, where Harry was to deliver a speech to a group of reserve officers. Their last stop in the East would be in New York, where they planned to visit Margaret and to attend a conference sponsored by the American Jewish Congress. The last time they had made a long-distance trip together by car was just after the Democratic Convention in 1944, when Harry had been nominated for Vice-President.

Their friends tried desperately to discourage them from making the more-than-thousand-mile journey. "Be sensible; go by train or plane," they pleaded. "After all, both of you are almost seventy!"

Bess and Harry remained unconvinced. "We're looking forward to it," Bess replied. "Besides, Harry wants to break in his new car."

The truth was that the automobile already had had some breaking in. Truman had only owned the car for a week when he scraped the chromium as he tried to go through the narrow gate on their driveway. "The boss bawled me out good," he said. "It only ended when a few days later she did exactly the same thing with her car. After that she never mentioned it again."

"They had hoped to travel incognito," said Truman's cousin, Mrs. Haukenberry. "But Harry's speedy driving helped spill the beans. They had discussed who would do the driving. He complained that she drove too slowly. She said that he drove too fast. They worked out a compromise—Harry would be behind the wheel, but he would drive slower than usual. They had only gone a short distance when Bess complained that he was speeding. He insisted that he was only doing fifty-five. 'Do you think I'm losing my eyesight?' Bess said. 'Slow down!'"

Truman wrote in his book, *Mr. Citizen,* that at fifty-five miles an hour other cars soon started passing them. "They had a chance to look us over," said the former President. "Pretty soon the shouted greetings started."

From then on the entire nation knew that the Trumans were driving to Washington. They were given police escorts, reporters tried to interview them during overnight stops, photographers mounted cameras on car roofs and followed close behind. Outside of Wheeling, West Virginia, one driver almost careened into them as he tossed a piece of paper through their open window and shouted for autographs.

"It's just like the old days," Bess complained. "This is the last time we go by car! I'll sure be glad when we get back to the tranquility of our house!"

It was anything but serene when they returned to Independence. As they pulled into their driveway, they saw a youngster kneeling in their garden pulling up roses. He didn't stop when Harry approached him. "Ma told me that you won't mind when you realize we want souvenirs." Before the startled Truman could reply, the lad climbed over the fence and ran to a waiting car.

Herbert Hoover had warned Bess and Harry about their house becoming a tourist attraction. "Nothing is sacred," the former President had cautioned. "Every single thing is considered a potential souvenir. A fence helps but it doesn't always keep trespassers out. I suppose the only cure is moving to a deserted island or learning to live with it."

Bess once confided to Ethel Noland, "I should feel flattered that they still want mementos. Nevertheless, sometimes I find myself wanting to shoo them away with a broom. The more persistent ones want to know if I miss living in the White House."

"That was the most common question that was posed to her," said Miss Noland. "Bess regularly received dozens of letters about it from inquisitive people. Reporters asked it regularly. Clerks in stores she shopped in were curious. Even many of her friends kept searching for telltale hints. Finally Bess did something she had never done before—she wrote an open letter to a lady in Iowa who also wanted to know. It was printed in newspapers all over the country."

> Certainly today I do. I have just spent the afternoon trying to find a yard man, but I had no luck. I do some of the gardening myself—we have lovely masses of flowers right now and I work hard at my roses. How nice it would be to have a few of those White House gardeners caring for our grounds.
>
> We have a power mower and I spent the better part of last summer trying to induce Mr. Truman to use it. Finally he did. Eleven o'clock of a Sunday morning, with all the Methodists and Baptists going by our house on the way to church, Mr. Truman got out on our front lawn in his shirt sleeves and began cutting the grass. When I looked out of the window and saw him, I was horrified.
>
> "Harry! Come in here this minute," I called to

him. "You know what those churchgoers are saying." There's no doubt in my mind he planned the whole thing deliberately to save himself from ever touching that mower again. And he hasn't.

Here in Independence we have a large, three-story house and it would be extremely pleasant to have some of the wonderful staff we had in the White House to help run it. I certainly miss them . . . Life [here] is easier, slower, much more relaxed. People smile more. We have the luxury of undemanded time, but we also have the occasional dullness that goes with it. I am not much of a joiner, never have been, and clubs take little of my time. I go to church regularly, play a little bridge. The mail is still mountainous, but I have no secretarial help, so when I get snowed under I send out an S.O.S. to Mr. Truman's office . . .

For the truth is, I have two loves, and I would be happiest if I could live half-time in Washington, and half-time in Independence. My husband and I lived in the Capital too long for us not to miss it fondly when we are away from it.

Shortly after Harry's seventieth birthday he and Bess attended an outdoor performance of *Call Me Madam* in Kansas City. During the second act he complained of a severe pain and said he was having trouble keeping his food down. An alarmed Bess helped him get into the car and drove back to Independence. She had to stop several times to allow him to vomit.

As soon as they arrived home, Bess sent for the doctor. His diagnosis was that the former President was suffering from a gall-bladder attack. The following morning Truman was taken to the Research Hospital in Kansas City, where he underwent surgery.

The operation to remove the gall bladder was a success. "Three things pulled me through," Harry claimed. "My tough physical condition, expert medical care and most important of all—Bess's constant attention!"

Pauline Krueger, a nurse, recalled how devotedly Bess catered to her husband. "The President had lots of medical attention," Mrs. Krueger said. "But she was really his chief nurse. She'd sit by his bed for hours not saying anything— just looking. That fond gaze was, as the Chinese say, worth a thousand words. When he was awake, she'd read to him. All sorts of things. On July Fourth it was the Declaration of Independence that appeared in a newspaper. She'd read a little and then he'd finish it off. It was like a game. Most of the time he got it right. When he didn't they'd both burst out laughing like a bunch of kids."

Harry amazed the staff by his rapid recovery, and he was released from the hospital well ahead of schedule. However, the doctors warned Bess that it would be at least a year before he would feel well enough to return to a normal routine.

"If I know Harry, it will be lots sooner," she replied confidently.

"As usual, Mother was right," Margaret said. "Within two months Dad was back to working six days a week."

When Bess was convinced that he was completely re-covered, she agreed to go with him to California, where he had been invited to deliver a series of lectures. Charles Murphy, who had been a leading member of the White House staff, accompanied them. "Mrs. Truman wanted to include Disneyland on their itinerary," he said. "She and I were for it. The President was vehemently opposed and delivered a fifteen-minute tirade on how it was only for children. 'Catch me going on those rides!' he blustered. So Mrs. Truman and I planned to go by ourselves. The following morning at breakfast she said something about our proposed trip. He perked up his ears and asked what we were talking about. 'Mr. Murphy and I are going to Disneyland tomorrow,' she replied.

"Later that day he held a press conference and the first question concerned his schedule. Very quickly he answered, 'Tomorrow I'm off for Disneyland!'

"The next day the three of us went, and I must say we all enjoyed it—the President the most. We tried out the rides. Mrs. Truman drew the line at the High Rise. The President and I went. He was delighted and kept telling her all about it."

While they were eating lunch in a Disneyland restaurant, the hostess came to their table and said that Drew Pearson was there and would like to join them. "To put it mildly," said Murphy, "the columnist and the Trumans were not on the best of terms."

Harry looked at Bess, who nodded affirmatively, at which point the ex-President said, "Okay. Bring him over."

It was a friendly visit. After it was over Bess said, "Harry, what did I tell you—Walt Disney draws out the best in people—especially adults. I'm going to take my grandchildren—if I ever have any—to Disneyland."

The Trumans were apprehensive about the possibility of Margaret never getting married. Once when they visited Lucy and Mize Peters, old friends who lived near them in Independence, Harry expressed their doubts to Mrs. Peters. "I envy you, Lucy, because you are a grandmother," he had said. "I'm afraid Margaret isn't going to marry but will follow the family pattern of my sister, my aunts and my cousins by the dozens."

XXI APPLE OF THEIR EYE

"NEVER HAVE I seen any parents closer to a child than were President and Mrs. Truman to Margaret," said Charles Ficklin, a White House butler. "She was not only the apple of their eyes, but to them she was the whole barrel—and all of it good!"

Margaret arrived on February 17, 1924, nearly five years after Bess and Harry were married. The baby's mother was thirty-nine years old, her father forty. "Both parents were ecstatic but unprepared," recalled Ethel Noland. "Margaret, who was born at home, came ahead of schedule, and a crib hadn't been bought yet. Bess's mother felt it was unlucky to buy things well ahead of time, so a dresser drawer had to be used."

Margaret says, "I don't mind having been cradled in a drawer. Many good actors and actresses say they got their start in life that way, and maybe that's the reason I have always been stagestruck."

The infant may not have had a proper place to sleep, but she already had dozens of devoted fans. "She was the first baby born to a Wallace in a long while," said Harry's cousin, Mrs. Haukenberry. "They all lived just a stone's throw away and saw her all the time. Margaret could easily have been spoiled. Providentially, Harry and Bess were determined to be sensible parents and saw to it that she had an orderly childhood. It wasn't always easy."

Margaret remembers those early years as being "extremely enjoyable ones." She once confided to anthropologist Margaret Mead, "I didn't succeed very often in playing one parent against the other—it was very rare that they disagreed. When I was very young my father came home at fairly regular hours except when he was out campaigning. He'd always play with me. He was my first piano teacher."

Dr. Mead pointed out that it was very unusual during that period for fathers to take such personal interest in a daughter's upbringing. That was when Margaret said, "I was the most joint product imaginable. Both of my parents were very close to me. Do you think it was because I was an only child?"

"No," Dr. Mead replied. "I doubt it. I don't believe it would have been very different if they had two or three children."

"People were always assuming that I must have spent a very lonely childhood, longing for a sister or brother," Margaret said. "Actually, I loved being an only child."

Mrs. George Wallace, Bess's sister-in-law, recalled, "They would spend hours discussing the best method of bringing up their very beautiful blonde daughter. They finally settled on a mixture of good old-fashioned common sense, the latest medical know-how and lots of love."

Once the conversation was about what to do with a cousin who had a chronic "runny nose" and insisted, nevertheless, on fondling baby Margaret. Bess, in her very practical way, suggested that they provide the woman with a gauze mask. "She'll soon get the idea that we don't want her nuzzling the child," she said.

Miss Noland remembered another time the Truman brand of child care produced positive results. She said, "It

was when three-year-old Margaret started to cry because a
playmate had snatched her favorite doll. She grabbed it
back. Soon the other youngster was doing the crying. That
was when Bess confiscated the doll and put each little girl at
an opposite end of the room. As soon as they stopped their
whimpering, she drove them to the ice cream parlor for
chocolate cones.

"She bought one for herself," Miss Noland added. "She
said she felt she deserved one for settling the doll dispute.
Bess could always find an excuse to eat chocolate cones!"

Bess continued to use this "sensible sugar" philosophy
when her daughter grew older. Once she took Margaret and
Drucie Snyder out to lunch. Drucie is one of Margaret's
closest friends and daughter of John Snyder. "In a sense
Mrs. Truman regarded me as her own daughter," said
Drucie, now Mrs. John Horton. "She was always picking us
up on our manners. We were sitting there having hot
chocolate, clutching the heavy cups. Suddenly Mrs. Truman
said, 'Margaret and Drucie, will you for heaven's sake hold
your cups properly?'

"I replied, 'Have you tried it? They're too heavy—you
can't do it!'

"'Then you should have ordered tea!' she said. 'It's
served in daintier cups!'

"I guess Margaret and I gave her problems. We'd hide
behind the plants and make faces. She'd reprimand us. But
always in a way we didn't object to. She'd be firm, but fair.
Never a smother-mother, if you know what I mean. She'd
always be loving, and you realized it quickly. That's a side
of her the public rarely saw. But in her private life it showed
up all the time. It always did. My mother and John, my
husband, were sitting around our house chatting on a
Sunday afternoon. Mrs. Truman was visiting. Suddenly my
four-year-old daughter asked my mother for a hankie and
walked over to the coffee table and proceeded to dust it off.
Dust rose in clouds. John and my mother were very
embarrassed.

"Mrs. Truman watched her. Then she said, 'Let her go right ahead, because it's obvious that no one else around here seems to do it.' This wasn't a caustic remark, but a loving one. She simply didn't want to see the child repri- manded.''

Mary Shaw Branton, another of Margaret's childhood friends, said, "I can't remember a time when I didn't know her. My mother and Mrs. Truman were boon companions and were so pleased when their daughters hit it off. From the time I was a little girl until this very day, I always knew where I stood with Mrs. Truman. That may well be the secret of her success. No deviousness—nothing hidden under the cover. I don't mean that if she doesn't approve of something she will start yelling. Perish the thought. However, you know instinctively when she's displeased— and you don't want to do it again.''

The summer Margaret was twelve she joined the Trinity Episcopal Church choir. Mrs. William Sermon, the direc- tor, told Bess that her daughter had a fine soprano voice that should be cultivated. "It was the beginning of my dream of becoming a famous opera star,'' Margaret re- vealed to Dr. Mead. "I started fantasying about wearing a beautiful, long white dress with a rose in my hair. I had all sorts of leading roles—frequently I was Mimi in *La Boheme*. The audience kept shouting '*bravissima*' as I threw the rose at my parents who were sitting in the front row.''

When Harry was elected to the Senate in 1934, Margaret was enrolled in Gunston Hall, a private school for girls in Washington. Half of the school year she'd spend there and the other half in the public school in Independence that her parents had attended fifty years before.

"She didn't seem to mind the changes and would always pick up just where she had left off,'' said Alex Petrovic, who moved on from that school to acquire the same Jackson County judge's seat that was Truman's when he first entered politics. Petrovic, who still lives in Missouri, was a classmate of Margaret's. He recalled, "I once appeared in a junior high school play with her. It was called *For Pete's Sake.* Billy Jones, who was also in the cast, was madly in love with Margaret. Remember this was in junior high—we were about fifteen at the time. Billy and I concocted a plot for him to kiss her. During the dress rehearsal I was to hold her while he did the smooching. At first everything went along as we had planned. But we hadn't counted on the prop Margaret had in her hand. It was a large plaster spoon. She hit us with it and the spoon broke into a thousand pieces. All at once everybody was gaping at us.

"'Why are you hitting those boys?' asked the faculty director. 'That's not in the script!'

"'They know full well!'

"Years later I told Mrs. Truman about the episode. She laughed and said, 'I hope Margaret didn't hurt you; stealing a kiss can produce loads of headaches. Particularly at age fifteen!'"

"Mother never gave me any sex education," said Bess's daughter to Dr. Mead. "It wasn't the sort of thing a lady did—just not proper. Certainly I wouldn't ask my father!"

In 1942 Margaret graduated from Gunston Hall. Jane Lingo, a school chum, said, "Gunston Hall prided itself on turning out polished Southern belles. I guess it didn't succeed with us. Don't get me wrong—it really was a fine place, but we both decided to attend a college that had both male and female students. We chose George Washington University, where we would be day students. Her parents were delighted. It meant that Margaret would continue living at home."

However, when the Trumans moved into the White House, their daughter's school troubles began:

A Secret Service agent observed her every move.

Answering routine questions in class often resulted in the replies being widely quoted as reflecting the latest administration thinking.

It was rumored that her written homework was prepared by an undersecretary of state.

The Hatchet, a student newspaper, ran a front-page story that was bannered: "Boss' Daughter Great Catch for Anyone." The Trumans were furious. One headline was narrowly avoided through the ingenuity of Margaret's history professor, Dr. Lowell J. Ragatz. Margaret's class was studying European alliances, and Margaret had selected Russia as her field of research. She was to present an oral report on her findings. Dr. Ragatz realized that whatever the President's daughter said on this sensitive subject might have international reverberations. He decided to hold the seminar in his own home and telephoned Mrs. Truman for approval. The First Lady agreed that it was a splendid idea, but suggested that it might be easier if the students met in the White House.

"The President and I will be upstairs, and you can have the downstairs," she said. "Just prepare a list of who will be along so the guards will let them in."

"I conducted the class in the State Dining Room," Dr. Ragatz said. "Margaret set out maps and a blackboard. Her report was an excellent one. Reporters, however, weren't privy to it."

Dating was another area that presented unwieldy situations. "You'd think being the President's daughter was a blessing," said White House maid Lillian Rogers Parks. "Well, it sure wasn't when it came to romance. Poor Margaret never knew if the boy really liked her for what she was or if he just wanted publicity. We used to feel so sorry for her and would shake our heads and mutter: 'There goes the sad little Princess.'

"Her father didn't help matters much, either. Whenever

he felt she was staying out too late on a date, he'd send the Secret Service to fetch her. Luckily for Margaret, Mrs. Truman was more relaxed on the subject. If not for her easing things up, the President would have interfered all the time. It was good that she wanted to make her way as a singer before she got married."

Although government and history had been Margaret's majors, upon receiving her B.A. degree she resolved that she'd go to New York and sing professionally. "My parents didn't stand in my way," she told Dr. Mead. "When I announced to them that I was planning to be a singer and an actress, they warned me that it was going to be difficult, but they didn't put obstacles in my path."

Lawrence Tibbett, a well-known opera baritone, heard Margaret sing. "She's good," he said. "But I fear that since she is the daughter of the President of the United States, critics will demand a lot more of her than they'd ask of plain Margaret Jones."

Spurred on by Tibbett's praise, Margaret started practicing in earnest. Her debut was postponed slightly when it was discovered that she was suffering from bronchial pneumonia. Penicillin was prescribed, and a week later, with a red nose and watery eyes, she appeared in her first concert. Accompanied by the Detroit Symphony Orchestra, she performed on NBC radio to an estimated audience of twenty million people. She sang a Spanish folk song, an aria from *La Perle du Brésil* and "The Last Rose of Summer."

"When I got back to the hotel," Margaret recalled, "I had a telephone call from Daddy, who told me that I had done wonderfully, but of course he was prejudiced. Mother said quietly that she was satisfied. By and large the critics were very kind to me. They may have been more kind than I deserved."

Most of them found her voice quite acceptable and predicted a promising future if she had more training and experience. For the next year Margaret practiced vigorously. When she felt she was good enough, she gave concerts around the country and abroad. She appeared regularly on radio and TV shows. Most of her performances drew favorable reviews. Her contract with NBC paid her from $2000 to $2500 a performance. Her total earnings were reported to exceed her father's annual Presidential salary. She said cheerfully on one radio show, "Well, a vocalist always makes more money than the accompanist."

Bess commented, "From now on Margaret pays her own way. As a matter of fact, I might even ask her for a loan."

Just before one tour Margaret was invited to appear on "Person to Person," a popular television program that showed celebrities in their own homes. Margaret was to substitute for host Ed Murrow, who was covering the British election. Her assignment was to interview Bess and Harry and have them take the viewing audience on a trip through the house in Independence. She sat in the New York studio and talked to her parents, who were at 219 North Delaware Street.

Former President Herbert Hoover saw the show and enjoyed it. "The 'Person to Person' program about the Trumans was one of my all-time favorites. . . . All of them looked quite dignified. As usual he was a bit brash, Mrs. Truman apprehensive and at times a bit economical of words. Margaret as bright as a button. On the whole they were quite natural."

Here are some excerpts from the show:

MARGARET:　　　　Ed Murrow wanted me to ask you just how much influence and help was mother when you were in the White House?

MR. TRUMAN:　　　She was a wonderful influence and help. A President is in a bad way if he doesn't have a First Lady that knows her job and is a full support to him.

	She's the greatest help a President can have. Mine was.
MRS. TRUMAN:	Thank you.
MARGARET:	Mother, let me switch from Washington to Kansas City. How is your baseball team doing?
MRS. TRUMAN:	We are doing very well. We are going to have a great team before the season is far gone.
MARGARET:	You're the sports fan of the family. Have you seen anything good on TV lately?
MRS. TRUMAN:	A few good things, yes. But I haven't been able to find a wrestling match—none at all.
MARGARET:	You know a lot of people have said to me, "Your father sure loves a fight." True or false?
MR. TRUMAN:	Well, I never promoted a fight, but I never ran from one if it was necessary to meet things head on.

[At this point Bess glanced quizzically at her husband.]

MARGARET:	Mommy, do you want to say a few words about politics specifically or in general?
MRS. TRUMAN:	No, not in either category, thank you.
MR. TRUMAN:	You know your mother never talks about such things.

[When Bess was walking from one room to another, she

started murmuring under her breath. Margaret said firmly, "No kibitzing!" The former First Lady looked puzzled but stopped her muttering. A few moments later her daughter asked her final question.]

MARGARET: There goes the clock. Mother, what advice do you have on raising children?

MRS. TRUMAN: Oh, absolutely none. Do you think I have had any luck?

Time magazine, which had never been known as one of Truman's great boosters, agreed with Herbert Hoover. Their TV critic wrote, "Although Bess and Harry failed to display the easy, unaffected stage presence of their daughter, the Trumans on the whole brought the show off in folksy fashion. Margaret was charming and her parents were dignified in one of "Person to Person"'s best shows yet."

Margaret spent the 1955 Christmas season with her parents in Independence. During the holidays she received a number of telegrams and bouquets of flowers from a Mr. Clifton Daniel. She had met the *New York Times* editor at a party the month before. "He looks like a silver-haired Lord Byron," a guest said. "As handsome as the poet and probably sounds like him, too."

Daniel was a persistent suitor. In January he proposed and Margaret accepted. She informed her mother and father that they were going to have a newspaperman for a son-in-law. Daniel fondly recalls his first meeting with his future in-laws. "The President and Mrs. Truman had come to New York for a few days," he said. "They were staying with their daughter at the Carlyle Hotel. Margaret asked us what we'd like to drink. They ordered bourbon and water. Margaret had sherry. I said, 'A glass of milk.'

"I'm told they were shocked and wondered what sort of a son-in-law they were getting. I had just returned from Russia, where I had been ill. An ulcer was suspected, and I was put on a bland diet. Hence the milk. The incident has since become a family joke."

On the afternoon of April 21, 1956, the couple were married in the same church Bess and Harry had been wed in thirty-seven years before. For the occasion the pews in the red-bricked Trinity Episcopal Church had been given fresh coats of beige and brown paint. The carpets had received a brisk scrubbing, and the pastor had purchased a new box of candles.

Hardly the equivalent of the gala international wedding newspapers were comparing it to. The other affair had just occurred in Monaco, where an assortment of royalty had watched His Serene Highness, Prince Rainier, take actress Grace Kelly as his bride. Then the regal guests were treated to an elaborate display of fireworks as they sipped vintage champagne aboard the prince's spectacular yacht.

In Independence as the minister pronounced the Truman-Daniel couple man and wife, Bess wiped her eyes and said, "Thank goodness this is Missouri, not Monaco." Then she rushed back to 219 North Delaware Street, where a reception was to be held.

After the last guest had left, she removed her shoes and said to Harry, "Everything went along smoothly, but why did Margaret have to get married on the opening day of the baseball season? There are 364 other days she could have chosen!"

Four handsome sons have resulted from the Truman-Daniel union, and Bess is as proud a grandmother as any. So proud, in fact, that when she went visiting, she'd never carry photographs of her grandchildren for fear that she would bore everybody by showing them all the time. However, she does differ in one area. Whereas most grandmothers privately believe that their grandsons will grow up to be President, she is opposed to Clif, Will, Harrison and Thomas Daniel serving for even one term.

She once told a member of her Independence bridge club, "Harry and I often discussed their futures. He used to say, 'The Presidency is a job that I wouldn't wish on anyone—let alone Margaret's boys. If they want to go into politics, let them be senators. That was the happiest time of my life.'"

XXII NEVER AGAIN PLAIN MR. AND MRS. CITIZEN

BESS AND HARRY agreed that having once occupied the White House it was hopeless to try to resume living normal lives. Truman said sadly, "After you've served as President of the United States, you can never again expect to be a plain, ordinary citizen. You can never escape some of the responsibilities of the Presidency. They follow you for as long as you live. And that goes for your family, too."

This "can never again" reasoning was clearly demonstrated during a trip the Trumans made to western Europe. With Margaret's wedding successfully behind them, Bess and Harry felt they had earned a much-needed holiday. When England's Oxford University announced that they wanted to present Truman with an honorary doctor of civil law degree, the decision was to vacation abroad. They carefully pored over travel folders, and after much debate they agreed upon an itinerary: Le Havre, Paris, Rome, Naples, Assisi, Florence, Venice, Salzburg, Munich, Bonn, Brussels, The Hague, London. "Harry was tremendously popular in Western Europe," Bess told Ethel Noland. "Long before Americans began revering him."

In May, 1956, the Trumans sailed for Le Havre aboard the liner *United States*. "It almost didn't come off," Harry recalled. "A few days before we left, I hurt my foot carrying a big load of stuff. The doctor diagnosed it as a mild sprain and said it would go away. But for a good part of our trip, I limped and had to depend almost completely on a cane."

When the Trumans returned to Independence two months later, Bess invited some of her neighbors over for tea to show them photographs and to tell them all about their holiday. "I suppose you could call it a thrilling time," she said. "We were wined and dined by the greats. Lunch with Queen Elizabeth at Buckingham Palace, a private audience with Pope Pius XII at the Vatican, a dinner at 10 Downing Street where the guests included Sir Winston Churchill, Prime Minister Anthony Eden and Earl Clement Attlee. We met slews of high dignitaries—Queen Juliana, Chancellor Konrad Adenauer, French President Coty. Prime Minister Nehru even made a special trip to London.

"Everybody was most charming, but still we rarely had a minute to ourselves. For instance in Venice, Harry and I took a gondola ride on the Grand Canal. It was a very romantic ride—half a dozen photographers followed close behind in another gondola!"

One of the neighbors wanted to know if it was true that the European hotels were cold. "That's a bit difficult to answer," Bess replied. "With my case of arthritis I never knew if there was a cool draft or if it was my feet that were acting up." Then she laughed and said, "Undoubtedly it was caused by my chilly stare. Perhaps I should have used it more often to frighten away some of the newsmen."

She felt the high point of the trip was when Harry was awarded his honorary degree at Oxford University. "For the occasion he had to wear a red coat and a Henry VIII–type of hat," she said. "A sort of sawed-off tophat with a tremendous brim. The students were so pleased with him they started cheering and chanting, 'Give 'em hell, *Harricum.*'"

Back at home the former President set about eagerly to supervising the construction of the Harry S. Truman Library, which was being built in Independence. It was to house all his papers—5½ million documents—and store tons of memorabilia he and Bess had accumulated. Also a room on the main floor was to be an exact replica of the White House Oval Office.

Bess knew the library was very much the focus of her husband's life. "I've never seen a person so anxious to see something completed," Bess told Mrs. Randall Jessee. "He all but did it himself. As you know, our house is just minutes away, and we'd drive over constantly to view the progress. One evening we visited after the workmen had left for the day and someone—a teenager, most likely—had printed on one wall in green chalk: 'I'm wild about Harry.' I remember how tickled he was, but he found a rag and scrubbed the wall clean. Then he said to me, 'Everything here has to be in apple pie order.'"

A year later they attended the dedication of the library. Next to the main doorway, chiseled in stone, are these words:

> This library will belong to the people of the United States. My papers will be the property of the people and be accessible to them. And this is as it should be. The papers of the Presidents are among the most valuable source materials for history. They ought to be preserved and they ought to be used.
>
> Harry S. Truman

In the silence following the invocation, dignitaries standing close to the former President heard him say to his wife, "There should be another name on it, Bess—yours!"

"He was very proud of the library," said Katie Loucheim, former chairwoman of the Women's Division of the Democratic National Committee. "He was always talking about it or showing it off. Somehow he'd manage to include Bess's name in conjunction with it. When he escorted me through the building, he stopped at a display that contained a sword inlaid with many precious stones. 'I told Bess that I'd give her the diamond in the sword,' he said, 'if she promised to get rid of Mr. Bricker for me!'*

"Once I heard him going over the plans for the administration of the library with Dean Acheson. In a loud voice the President said, 'As the executor, you should know that I want to be buried right there.' He pointed to the rose garden on the library grounds. 'Mrs. Truman is to be buried next to me. Take care of that matter!'

"Acheson replied, 'I don't like to discuss those unpleasant things, but I agree. Because I know full well that if I don't do exactly as you say, you'll probably haunt me.'

"The President grinned and nodded. 'You're damn right I will!' he said."

In the spring of the following year, Truman and comedian Jack Benny appeared together on the stage of the Kansas City Municipal Auditorium. They were giving a benefit concert to help raise money for the local symphony orchestra. During rehearsals Harry and Jack traded quips. "For a President he's a pretty good stand-up comic," Benny remarked. "However, the prize for one-liners goes to his wife, who put her hands over her ears when she heard us play—Harry on the piano, me with the violin. 'Only a mother could appreciate that music,' she gasped, 'a stone-deaf one!'"

*John Bricker, a Republican senator from Ohio, was a constant source of irritation to Truman. He was Harry's Vice-Presidential opponent in the '44 election and failed to concede defeat or send a congratulatory telegram.

After the concert the Trumans attended a social gathering. Harry was standing in the corner of the room, regaling the male guests with some of his fanciful tales. A woman seated next to Bess said wistfully, "I sure wish we could hear those stories."

"Don't bother," the former First Lady replied. "'I've heard them all. We aren't missing anything."

Come summer, the Trumans planned another trip to Europe. This time they desperately tried to avoid the press and instructed Rose Conway, Harry's secretary, not to release any advance information. The U.S. government was ahead of her. A high-ranking State Department official learned of their plans and promptly leaked the news to columnist Drew Pearson, who coyly asked, "What former President and First Lady are sailing to gay Paree aboard the American Export Liner *Independence?*"

It was a quick trip, and no top-level entertaining was scheduled. They nearly succeeded in appearing as they wished—"a couple of tourists from Mizzou."

During a one-day stopover in Rome, Harry asked a desk clerk for the name of a first-rate native restaurant. *"Palazzi,"* the man quickly replied. "It's a very fine villa on the outskirts of the town that has been turned into an elegant eating place. It overlooks much of the city and the food is magnificent."

Bess and Harry were delighted—until a State Department representative showed up and shook his head. "You can't possibly go to such a place," he warned. "Mussolini built it for his mistress, Clara Petacci. Think how it would look in the press if it got out that the former President and his wife frequented the villa of Mussolini's mistress during their one night in Rome!"

Harry was disappointed, but agreed that it might not be such a good idea. Bess, who usually kept her opinions to herself in public, thought a moment, then said, "Well, after all, *she* won't be there."

That night the Trumans dined at the Palazzi, where an editor of a leading Italian magazine came over to their table and asked Bess to write an article for his publication. "No, thank you," she replied. "Two ham writers in the family are enough." (Harry and Margaret had written and published books—see bibliography.)

The Trumans were home but had scarcely unpacked a suitcase before Harry was asked to be the principal speaker at a $25-a-plate luncheon at Washington's Mayflower Hotel. In his off-the-cuff talk, the former President cautioned his fellow Democrats not to go around wearing happy-days-are-here-again smiles and possessing too much confidence in the coming election.

Bess echoed her husband's fears of overoptimism, and when the chairman said that Bess's appearance had helped put life into the Party, she whispered to his wife, "I don't think the Democrats need any more life put into them. They got too much now!"

In May, after a quiet winter, Bess entered Research Hospital in Kansas City for a routine checkup. She was seventy-four years old and her only complaint was a stubborn cold. An examination revealed a tumor in her left breast. Dr. Wallace Graham, the family physician and former White House chief medical practitioner, advised an immediate operation. This was done.

"The President refused to budge from the bedside," said a night nurse. "You see devoted spouses all the time, but this one took the cake. You practically had to cut him loose with a saw!"

A greatly relieved Harry told the happy result of the biopsy to his wife. "No malignancy!" he said.

"Thank God," she replied. "I didn't want to go through the rest of my life with people feeling sorry for me."

A few hours later Bess heard more good news—she had become a grandmother for the second time. Daughter Margaret had just given birth to another son.

When Harry was convinced that Bess was fully recovered, he started campaigning for Kennedy in his usual bouncy style. In a speech he gave in San Antonio, Texas, he was quoted by the Associated Press as saying that anyone who voted for Nixon and Lodge "ought to go to hell" and that Nixon "never told the truth in his life."

Truman wondered afterward whether he had actually made the first statement, but added, "They can't challenge the second." He told a reporter, "You got me in lots of hot water with the boss. She gave me plenty of hell for making those remarks. What's all the fuss? After all, I didn't call him an S.O.B. because he insists he's a self-made man! You know that's a lie—Eisenhower made him!"

Randall Jessee, a family friend, said, "The Trumans were jubilant when Kennedy beat Nixon. They hadn't been his staunchest admirers when he first sought the office. I remember once Mr. Truman joked, 'It's not the pope I fear but the pop.'

"Mrs. Truman looked shocked. 'Harry, you ought not have said that,' she reproached him. 'Whatever am I going to do with you?'

"However, once Kennedy became the official Democratic candidate, there were no ifs or buts—he was their man!"

The new President invited the Trumans, their daughter and son-in-law to the White House. Bess, looking trimmer and happier than when she had lived in the Executive Mansion, complimented Jackie Kennedy on the changes she had made. "They are beautiful," Bess said. "I wish I had thought of them. And the dinner was delicious, though somewhat different from what I had served."

Clifton Daniel well remembers that dinner. "As usual, my mother-in-law was being very kind," he said. "That meal had some very amusing sidelights."

Daniel's newspaper colleagues considered him very knowledgeable about continental food. "I believe the dinner was prepared by the French chef the First Lady had hired," he recalled. "It was very elaborate in the usual

French style. The meal opened with a clear soup and a hot fish dish. The main course was grouse. The bird was tough. I tried to cut it and it jumped two feet away. I looked around at the other guests. Everybody had similar problems. Margaret, who was sitting at the head table opposite President Kennedy, heard him giving the devil to his wife because the bird was so tough. That's when Margaret came to the rescue. She turned to Bobby Kennedy, who was seated beside her, and said loudly, 'Those White House knives never could cut anything.'"

Bess tried to be polite and lifted the napkin to her mouth. However, it didn't entirely succeed in muffling her giggles. Soon everybody was laughing. As Bess left the dining room, a butler who had served the Truman family when they lived there temporarily forgot White House rules of conduct and softly applauded the former First Lady. Jackie noticed the incident but didn't scold the butler. She had often said that the First Lady she admired most was Bess Truman.

The President's mother, Rose Kennedy, told of another occurrence that revealed her daughter-in-law's feelings about Bess. "She was scheduled to talk to a reporter," said the Kennedy matriarch. "On the day of the interview, Jackie was too ill to see the writer, so Jack pinch-hit. 'My wife has a White House idol,' he said. 'It's Bess Truman, because being the President's wife didn't make her shed her values or spoil her daughter amidst all the glamour of the Executive Mansion. Jackie hopes to emulate her.'"

"The Trumans were genuinely grieved when President Kennedy was assassinated," said Jessee. "They felt that he had insufficient time to carry out his plans, but that the country was secure in the hands of Lyndon Johnson, his successor."

One of the first things the new President did when he was sworn in was phone Truman in Independence. Harry wished him well and hoped that when he found the time, he'd visit the library. Two years later Johnson accepted the invitation and flew to Independence.

"It was an emotional meeting," Lady Bird Johnson recalled. "Lyndon loved that man. And I felt it was mutual. As Mrs. Truman and I looked on, the two Presidents greeted each other with loads of respect and affection."

Mrs. Johnson wrote in her diary:

> When lunch was over, Mrs. Truman announced firmly (and I would have been shocked if he had countermanded her order) that she was going to take President Truman home now, his legs were wearing out a bit. We all said goodby, with many thanks, and I, especially, thinking how glad I would be someday to be in their shoes, to look so calm and content and happy as old age approached.

On their fiftieth wedding anniversary—June 28, 1969—a frail-looking eighty-five-year-old Truman repeated something he had said many times before: "Three things can ruin a husband—money, power and women. I never had money, I never wanted power and the only woman in my life is sitting beside me right now."

Bess blushed and once again said, "Harry, you ought not have said that." This time she added, "—in public." Then, trying to be as unobtrusive as possible, she brushed her right hand against his.

Donald Slusher, the mayor of Independence, sent them fifty red roses on behalf of all the citizens. Bess's Tuesday bridge club arranged for a florist to deliver fifty white carnations with gold-tinted leaves. Students from the local high school serenaded them. Bess was overwhelmed and said, "I always thought we'd have a garden party when the time came to celebrate our golden wedding anniversary. But Mr. Truman just isn't up to any of the hand-shaking it would take."

On Harry's eighty-seventh birthday, President Nixon wanted to present him with the Congressional Medal of

Honor. Nixon liked to be compared with the peppery little antihero of American politics and often remarked that he was the "Truman of the seventies." He told a group of bankers, "President Truman and I came out of similar humble backgrounds and by sheer grit pulled ourselves up by our own bootstraps. We are two of a kind—we both possessed moxie."

Bess laughed when she was told about his statement. "The only thing Harry and Nixon have in common is that they both play the piano. And from what I'm told, Harry's playing is much better."

Harry refused the medal. In a letter to his congressman, he wrote: "I do not consider that I have done anything which should be the reason for any award, congressional or otherwise." He wanted to add a postscript, but Bess didn't let him. It was: "Consider giving it to Mrs. Truman. She deserves it."

The death of the former President on the morning of December 26, 1972, ended one of the closest twentieth century partnerships the country has known. After a twenty-two-day battle against age and disease, Truman's heart failed. At the time a very weary Bess was at home—doctors and nurses literally had forced her to leave her husband's bedside for a brief rest. The official reason given for the death was: "A complexity of organic failure causing a collapse of the cardiovascular system."

President Nixon declared a national day of mourning and flew to Independence to lay a wreath on the coffin and offer his personal condolences to the widow. (Harry might well have chuckled at a rumor that wreath contained sprigs of poison ivy, which gave Nixon's hands the itch.)

At the services Bess walked slowly, carrying a cane but not using it for assistance. She was solemn but seemed self-contained. "I don't want to detract from the way Jackie conducted herself at President Kennedy's funeral," said

Drucie Snyder Horton. "But those of us who were privileged to observe Mrs. Truman's sweet, sad dignity will always feel it can never be topped."

As Bess left the rose garden, to the soft chimes of the carillon playing "Liberty Bell," a slight smile crossed her lips. Randall Jessee, who was acting as the family spokesman, said the smile was due to something Harry had once told her: "I would like to be buried out there so that I can get up and walk to my office if I want to. And when the time comes, you'll be there beside me, probably saying, 'Harry, you oughtn't!'"

XXIII BESS ALONE

AFTER TRUMAN'S DEATH, Margaret wanted Bess to come and live with her. "I prefer to be by myself!" the former First Lady replied.

Her daughter knew that no amount of pleading would help. "Once Mother decides on something important," she said, "nothing will budge her. However, she will most likely veto your suggestion with a kind and amusing remark."

Christine Sadler Coe, author of *America's First Ladies* and long-time Washington correspondent for *McCall's* magazine, said, "I overheard Margaret saying, 'Please move East and live with me.' Mrs. Truman replied in her typical dry-humor way, 'I always knew I was going to have trouble with you.'"

Bess continued to live at 219 North Delaware Street in Independence. "I was born here and hope to die here," she told a neighbor. "Unfortunately, these days not too many people are in a position to do that."

As a President's widow, she was entitled to an annual pension of $20,000. She was also the principal beneficiary of the $600,000 estate her husband had amassed from the sale of his published memoirs. "Up until then Harry and Bess never had what you could call wealth," said Mrs. Haukenberry. "He was probably the last poor man who will ever be elected President of the United States. At times it was tough sledding for them, but never once did anyone in the family hear them complain. It seemed that having each other and then Margaret was compensation enough."

One of the first things Bess said after the funeral was that she had indeed been blessed with luck to have married such a "good man." Then she quickly changed the subject. "Mrs. Truman has always been utterly considerate of other people's feelings," said Drucie Snyder Horton. "If she thinks you are depressed, she'll go out of her way to lift your spirits. I remember we were sitting in the library of her house following the President's funeral and I asked her if there was anything I could do for her.

"'Yes,' she replied. 'Why don't you read the newspapers and tell me what else happened today?' I mentioned that one story was about Howard Hughes's sudden disappearance. 'You know,' she said, 'I wonder if there really is a Howard Hughes? I think the newspapers invented him.' Here she was, distressed by her husband's death, but she felt we were the ones who needed some levity."

Drucie Horton's father, John Snyder, agreed with his daughter. "Bess would rather do things for you," he said, "than have things done for her." Snyder phones her in Independence at least once a month. He recalled one of the conversations:

> "Bess, how are you?"
> "Just fine."
> "Anything I can do?"
> "Nothing, thanks. Anything I can do for you?"
> "This is not just idle talk. If there is anything please let me know."
> "John, the only thing that bothers me a little is that it seems to me that this place is suddenly lots bigger than it used to be. But enough about me— is there anything you need?"

For the first few years following Harry's death, Bess lived alone in the fourteen-room house. Her arthritis bothered her, especially in her right knee, but she refused to have sleep-in help. Two women came in during the day—one to do the cleaning and the other to help with the cooking. Bess prepared her own breakfast, lighter fare than she had shared with her hearty-eating husband, and her own lunch, too, except when she had guests. A handyman did the outside chores. A Secret Service detail was stationed in a cottage across the street. One of the agents would drive the former First Lady to and from her errands.

"She should have somebody with her all the time," a neighbor said. "But she's afraid that person might talk her head off and figures that would be worse than no one at all."

Weather permitting, she still did her own shopping at Milgram's Supermarket on 24 Highway and kept weekly appointments at Doris Miller's beauty shop on West Maple. She made several visits to Margaret's home, entertained her grandsons with whimsical stories about their grandfather and then returned to Independence.

When the arthritis acted up, she would place the phone next to her chair and carry on extended conversations with friends and relatives, many of whom were similarly incapacitated. The more agile ones called in person. Randall Jessee said, "Mrs. Truman manages to get to the door with the aid of a cane and smilingly greets you. If it's possible she's even more gracious than ever. She's the only lady I know who writes a thank-you note for each Christmas card she receives—and done in a beautiful hand. She's abreast of current events; her knowledge of what's happening in the world is truly amazing. She keeps up with all the vetoes and legislation in Congress."

The few times Bess's name appeared in the press usually were related to her birthdays. One of the exceptions occurred in 1974, when she accepted the honorary cochairmanship for the reelection of Missouri Senator Thomas

Eagleton. The other cochairman was Stan Musial, a former
baseball star of the St. Louis Cardinals.

"Just imagine my name being linked with his," she said to
Harold Manning, a delivery boy. "Mr. Musial has a lifetime
batting average of .331. Seven times he led the league in
hitting. What company to be in!"

"She's like that," said Katie Louchheim. "She acts as if
she's the least important of the lot and that she has been privileged to rub shoulders with what she calls the real high and
mighty. Up until three years ago I used to call her regularly. It
was usually on Sunday morning and I'd try to keep the
conversation brief so that she wouldn't be late for church. One
morning she said to me, "Katie, now you can talk all you want
to. I don't go to church anymore because I can't kneel."

"I was quite startled. 'Mrs. T., I'm sure they don't expect
you to kneel!' I replied.

"'Katie, you don't know those Episcopalians!'"

Post-Watergate sentiment gave rise to a wave of nostalgia
for Truman's down-home honesty. Bess was thrilled when
she heard a famous rock group sing one of their hit songs:
"America Needs You, Harry Truman." Soon bumper
stickers and T-shirts started appearing sporting the same
plea. That was when the former First Lady said wistfully to
a friend, "Perhaps even more than America, I need him!"

The severity of her arthritis and several hospital trips
finally forced her to make changes. She surrendered the
upstairs bedroom she had shared with her husband and
moved to more convenient sleeping quarters on the ground
floor. And Margaret finally convinced her that she needed
around-the-clock help.

On May 8, 1976, which would have been Truman's
ninety-second birthday, President Ford and his wife visited
Bess. They were in Independence to attend the dedication
ceremony for a nine-foot bronze statue of the late President, which had been erected in the town square. His
ninety-one-year-old widow did not attend the tribute to her

husband, and the Fords called at 219 North Delaware Street.

Upon leaving the then First Lady said, "Imagine, she apologized for not answering the door personally. What a stoic woman. I've always been a Harry-and-Bess fan. You have to realize that Truman was President when we moved to Washington. He and the First Lady were so kind to us. She particularly—I'll never forget her many kindnesses. When Jerry got the Vice-Presidential nomination, she told me she let out a shriek of joy."

Mrs. Ford's sentiment is shared by Rosalynn Carter. "Since Jimmy and I have lived in the White House, I keep hearing things about Bess Truman," she said. "Marvelous things. She was without a doubt one of the most beloved occupants here."

Biographical statistics of living wives of American Presidents are always listed in *Who's Who*. The descriptive material is customarily furnished by the First Ladies themselves. Of the last eight women who held that post, Eleanor Roosevelt led with thirty-five lines. Then came Lady Bird Johnson, thirty-one; Jackie Kennedy Onassis, sixteen; Betty Ford, sixteen; Pat Nixon, twelve; Rosalynn Carter, twelve; Mamie Eisenhower, eleven. Bess is in last place with six lines. This is her entire entry in the 1978–79 edition:

> Truman, Bess Wallace (Mrs. Harry S. Truman). Wife of former pres. U.S.; b. Independence, Mo., Feb. 13, 1885, grad. high sch.; student Barstow Sch. for Girls, Kansas City, Mo.; Mr. Harry S Truman, June 28, 1919 (dec. Dec. 26, 1972), 1 dau.; Mary Margaret (Mrs. E. Clifton Daniel, Jr.); Democrat.

"It was like pulling teeth to get that much out of her," said one of the *Who's Who* editors. "That lady genuinely seeks anonymity."

Bess spent last February 13 quietly. She received a traditional congratulatory phone call from Margaret, who had visited her several weeks before; a bouquet of red carnations from the surviving members of "Captain Harry's" Battery D; and dozens of birthday cards from well-wishers. After carefully looking at all of them, she reached for the mystery novel she had been reading. Her passion for whodunits has not slackened over the years, and she quickly guessed the identity of the culprit.

Recently the ninety-five-year-old former First Lady was given an autographed copy of a brand new best-selling shocker called *Murder at the White House*. This whodunit was penned by her daughter and is about a secretary of state who has been murdered in the Executive Mansion. Everyone, including the President and his wife, are suspects. Upon learning of the plot Bess remarked, "Even as a child, Margaret had a vivid imagination. Besides, the wives of Presidents are much too busy to commit murder. The nearest I ever came to it was to wish occasionally that somebody or other had never been born."

It's difficult to find the proper definitive word for this uncommon common woman. Perhaps the most fitting is that Bess Truman is a democrat—with a small *d*. She is one of those rare persons who doesn't have two sets of manners but unfailingly treats everyone with the same degree of consideration and respect—and she does this without ever allowing herself to be imposed upon.

When she was offered this compliment it elicited a jovial response: "Oh, no, lots of people do that. For instance, there was Harry. He didn't hesitate to give heck to anybody."

BIBLIOGRAPHY

Acheson, Dean. *Present At the Creation.* New York: W. W. Norton, 1969.

Allen, Robert S., and Shannon, William V. *The Truman Merry-Go-Round.* New York: Vanguard, 1950.

Anderson, Patrick. *The Presidents' Men.* New York: Doubleday, 1968.

Barkley, Alben W. *That Reminds Me.* New York: Doubleday, 1954.

Bishop, Jim. *FDR's Last Year.* New York: William Morrow, 1974.

Blum, John Morton. *The Price of Vision.* Boston: Houghton Mifflin, 1973.

Byrnes, James. *Speaking Frankly.* New York: Harper, 1947.

Cochran, Bert. *Harry Truman and the Crisis Presidency.* New York: Funk & Wagnalls, 1973.

Daniels, Jonathan. *The Man of Independence.* Philadelphia: J. B. Lippincott, 1950.

Dayton, Eldorous L. *Give 'Em Hell Harry.* New York: Devain-Adair, 1956.

Donovan, Robert J. *Conflict of Crises.* New York: W. W. Norton, 1977.

Dorough, C. Dwight. *Mr. Sam.* New York: Random House, 1962.

Douglas, William O. *Go East, Young Man.* New York: Random House, 1974.

Edwards, India. *Pulling No Punches.* New York: Putnam, 1977.

Fields, Alonzo. *My 21 Years in the White House.* New York: Coward-McCann, 1961.

Fogleman, Edwin. *Hiroshima: The Decision to Use the A-Bomb.* New York: Scribner, 1964.

Ford, Betty. *The Times of My Life.* New York: Harper and Row, 1978.

Furman, Bess. *Washington By-Line.* New York: Knopf, 1949.

————. *White House Profile.* New York: Bobbs-Merrill, 1951.

Goldman, Eric F. *The Crucial Decade.* New York: Knopf, 1956.

Helm, Edith. *The Captains and the Kings.* New York: Putnam, 1954.

Hillman, William. *Mr. President.* New York: Farrar, Straus and Young, 1952.

Johnson, Haynes, and Johnson, Frank. *The Working White House.* New York: Praeger, 1975.

Johnson, Lady Bird. *A White House Diary.* New York: Holt, Rinehart and Winston, 1970.

Kirkendall, Richard S. *The Truman Period as a Research Field.* Columbia: University of Missouri Press, 1967.

Louchheim, Katie. *By the Political Sea.* New York: Doubleday, 1970.

Manchester, William. *The Glory and the Dream.* Boston: Little, Brown, 1973.

Means, Marianne. *The Woman in the White House.* New York: Random House, 1963.

Miller, Hope Ridings. *Embassy Row: Life and Times of Diplomatic Washington.* New York: Holt, Rinehart and Winston, 1966.

Miller, Merle. *Plain Speaking.* New York: Putnam, 1973.

Montgomery, Ruth. *Hail to the Chiefs*. New York: Coward-McCann, 1970.

Parks, Lillian Rogers. *Backstairs at the White House*. New York: Fleet Press, 1961.

Rigdon, William. *White House Sailor*. New York: Doubleday, 1962.

Robbins, Charles, and Smith, Bradley. *Last of His Kind*. New York: William Morrow, 1979.

Rosenman, Samuel and Dorothy. *Presidential Style*. New York: Harper and Row, 1976.

St. Johns, Adela. *Some Are Born Great*. New York: Doubleday, 1974.

Smith, A. Merriman. *Thank You, Mr. President*. New York: Harper, 1946.

———. *A President Is Many Men*. New York: Harper, 1948.

Smith, Marie D. *Entertaining in the White House*. Washington, D.C.: Acropolis, 1967.

Steinberg, Alfred. *The Man from Missouri*. New York: Putnam, 1962.

———. *Sam Rayburn*. New York: Hawthorn, 1975.

Talese, Gay. *The Kingdom and the Power*. New York: World, 1969.

Taylor, Tim. *The Book of Presidents*. New York: Arno Press, 1972.

Truman, Harry S. *Memoirs: Year of Decision*. New York: Doubleday, 1955.

———. *Memoirs: Years of Trial and Hope*. New York: Doubleday, 1956.

———. *Mr. Citizen*. New York: Bernard Geis, 1960.

Truman, Margaret. *Souvenir*. New York: McGraw-Hill, 1956.

———. *Harry S. Truman*. New York: William Morrow, 1973.

West, J. B. *Upstairs at the White House*. New York: Coward, McCann & Geoghegan, 1973.